The Scarbor(Companion

Things to do at little or no cost around Scarborough

Compiled by
Christopher More

First Published in the United Kingdom by Christopher More

ISBN 978-0-9557795-0-3

3 Glaves Paddock
Staxton
Scarborough
North Yorkshire
England YO12 4SX
www.scabbydonkey.com

A detailed guide covering the Scarborough and Filey area

Robin Hoods Bay to Flamborough
Scarborough to Malton
and all areas between

Introduction

Most of the printed guides available to the casual visitor to the Scarborough area are produced by publishers with a view to promoting advertising space within their covers.   This guide is intended to be different in that, there is no advertising and all the bias of the entries within this book are those places not generally listed within commercial publications.

The guide is written with the wealth of knowledge of a local writer who has spent a lifetime in the area and knows all those 'secret' places, some of which even locals may be unaware exist.

The guide is quite expensive to purchase when compared with the free leaflets found in information centres, however, the author guarantees that the purchase price of this guide will be re-payed many times over when readers realise just how many places can be visited in our area free of charge or at a modest (usually car parking) charge.

Many of the places listed are not on the usual tourist routes and are often only objects of passing to the unknowing, but, with a little historical reference these places can be brought to life and are then seen in a different light.

Several places included have volumous histories, but these entries have been kept to no greater than one page in this book and it is left to the individual reader to find further information if a particular reference is of interest.

The author welcomes feedback, good or bad, in order to keep this guide in a continual state of update and would be grateful for advice on inclusion of new entries.

Please take care when visiting outdoor locations, many of the locations listed are not 'normal' tourist places and as such are not necessarily over endowed with safety features that today's visitor is used to expect.

To make the most of your visit it would be advisable to purchase the Ordnance Survey OL27 map which is available from most book stores and some gift shops.

Contents

Cover picture: View above Goathland

Maps

Scarborough Area North

Scarborough Area South

Scarborough Town

Filey Town

Maps are simplified, not to scale, and are provided as a general reference.

Please use in conjunction with detailed local maps.

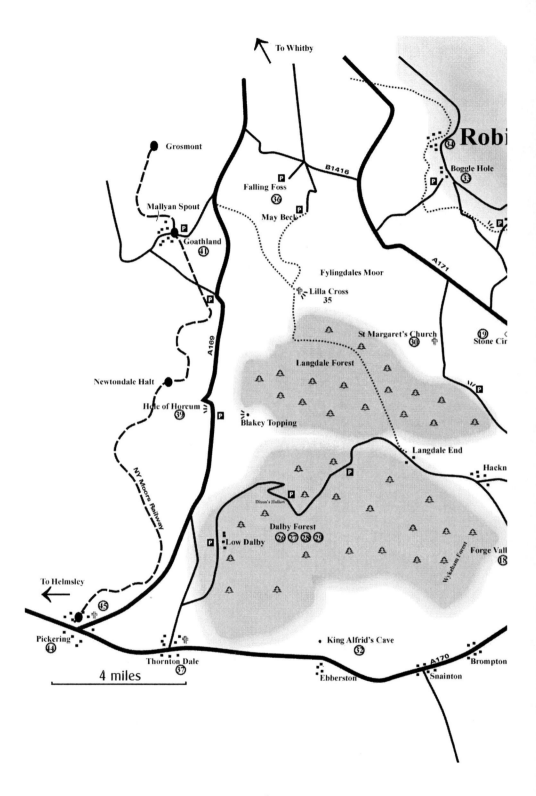

To Whitby

Grosmont

B1416

Falling Foss
36

May Beck

Mallyan Spout

Goathland
41

Fylingdales Moor

Lilla Cross
35

St Margaret's Church
30

Stone Cir

19

Langdale Forest

Newtondale Halt

A169

Hole of Horcum
39

Blakey Topping

Langdale End

Hackn

Dixon's Hollow

Dalby Forest
26 27 28 29

Low Dalby

Wykeham Forest

Forge Vall
18

NY Moors Railway

To Helmsley

45

King Alfrid's Cave
32

Pickering
44

Thornton Dale
37

4 miles

Ebberston

Snainton

A170

Brompton

Robi

Boggle Hole
33

34

A171

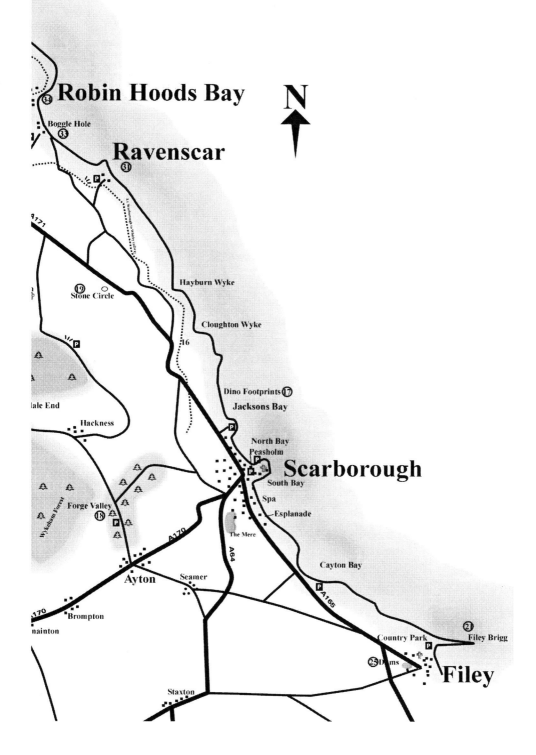

Robin Hoods Bay
Boggle Hole
Ravenscar
Hayburn Wyke
Stone Circle
Cloughton Wyke
16
Dino Footprints
Jacksons Bay
dale End
Hackness
North Bay
Peasholm
Scarborough
South Bay
Forge Valley
Spa
Esplanade
The Mere
Cayton Bay
Ayton
Seamer
Brompton
Country Park
Filey Brigg
nainton
Staxton
Dams
Filey

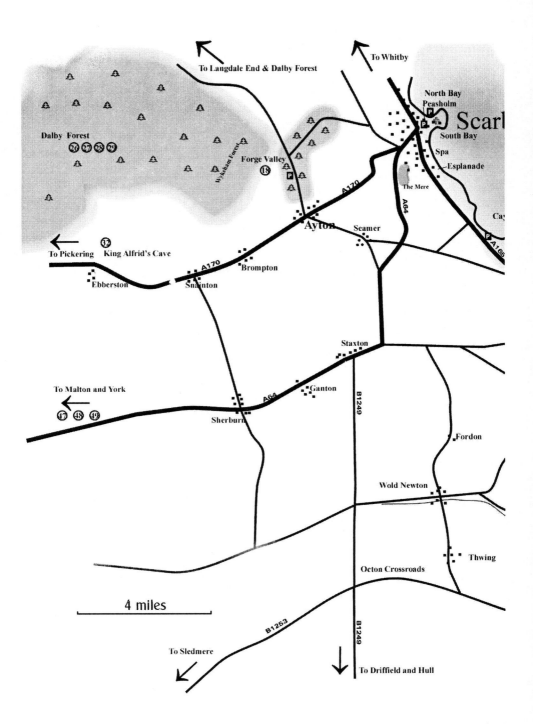

To Langdale End & Dalby Forest

To Whitby

North Bay
Peasholm

Scarl

Dalby Forest

South Bay

Wykeham Forest

Spa

Forge Valley

Esplanade

A170

The Mere

A64

Ayton

Seamer

Cay

To Pickering   King Alfrid's Cave

A170

A165

Ebberston

Snainton

Brompton

Staxton

To Malton and York

A64

Ganton

B1249

Sherburn

Fordon

Wold Newton

Thwing

Octon Crossroads

4 miles

B1253

B1249

To Sledmere

B1249

To Driffield and Hull

N

Scarborough
Bay

Esplanade

Cayton Bay

A165

Country Park
P
Dams
Filey Brigg
Filey

A165

Hunmanby

Gordon

B1229
RSPB
68
P
Flamborough

A165

Burton Fleming
Bempton
Danes Dyke
North Landing
P

Thwing
The Gypsey Race
42
P
Sewick Bay
P

Rudston Monolith
40
B1253
Sewerby
43
P
46
Sewerby Hall
South Landing

Rudston

Bridlington

P

9

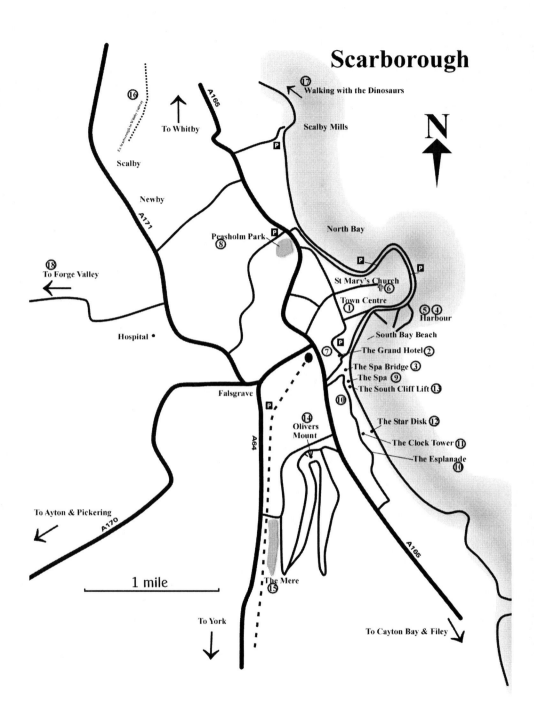

Scarborough

N

To Whitby

A165

17 Walking with the Dinosaurs

Scalby Mills

16

Scalby

Newby

A171

Peasholm Park
8

P

North Bay

P

P

18
To Forge Valley

St Mary's Church
6

Town Centre
1

5 4
Harbour

South Bay Beach

Hospital •

P

7

The Grand Hotel 2

The Spa Bridge 3

The Spa 9

The South Cliff Lift 13

Falsgrave

P

A64

14
Olivers
Mount

10

The Star Disk 12

The Clock Tower 11

The Esplanade
10

To Ayton & Pickering

A170

1 mile

A165

The Mere
15

To York

To Cayton Bay & Filey

10

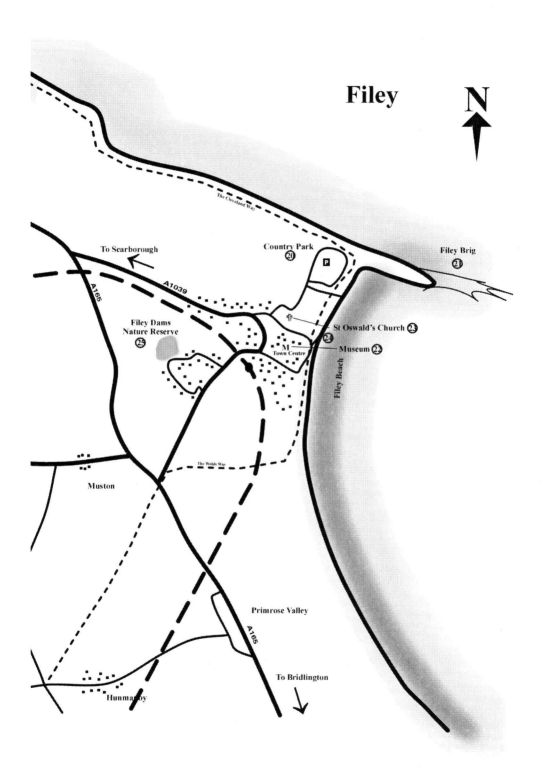

Filey

N

To Scarborough

Country Park 20

Filey Brig 21

P

A1039

A165

The Cleveland Way

Filey Dams
Nature Reserve 25

St Oswald's Church 23

24

M
Town Centre

Museum 22

Filey Beach

The Wolds Way

Muston

Primrose Valley

A165

To Bridlington

Hunmanby

Guide Entries

The entries that follow are listed in order of distance from Scarborough town centre.

Each entry is shown on the maps on pages 6-11 with the number marked in the summary pane.

Scarborough Town Centre

Scarborough town centre has suffered ,along with most other town centres throughout the country, with the replacement of older properties with modern more easy to maintain premises. The main street is very much like any town high street with the usual brand names dominating prime positions.

Huntriss Row

Cost	Free (Parking charges apply)
Time	Allow 3 hour plus
Parking	Town Centre P&D or Park & Ride

①

However, a few streets retain the warmth and charm of olden times and a visit to these will find small local businesses flourishing.

Two streets in particular are worth visiting. Huntriss Row with it's collection of Jewelers, Cafes and small retailers, and running parallel, Bar Street, with a similar selection of smaller shops, cafes and the like.

Also take time to visit the Market Vaults situated beneath Scarborough's early Victorian indoor market. In here you will find a collection of small retailers selling anything from picture framing to aromatic oils. This area was in disuse for many years and recently was improved, revitalised and opened up to small traders and start up businesses. It is now a flourishing area.

On St. Nicholas Street can be found the Town Hall, which, was originally built for a wealthy local banker in 1852 in an Elizabethan style. It became the town hall in 1900 and was greatly extended, as a local history book puts it, "in the same uncomfortable style". In front of the building is a statue of a Her Majesty Queen Victoria. This is a replica of one on Blackfriars Bridge in London and was erected in 1903. Surprisingly, Queen Victoria never visited Scarborough.

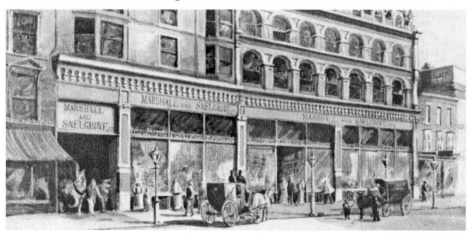

St Nicholas Street in the late 1900's, now, The Blue Lounge.

14

The Grand Hotel

At the north end of the Spa bridge can be found the most majestic hotel in Scarborough,
The Grand Hotel. Building started in 1863 to create a magnificent hotel to cater for the increasing number of wealthy visitors making use of the town and spa's facilities. Completed in 1867 to the design of Cuthbert Brodrick the structure in its original concept was supposed to have 4 Towers, 12 floors, 52 Chimneys and 365 rooms, to mimic the seasons, months, weeks and days of the year, although it would appear this did not work out exactly as planned.

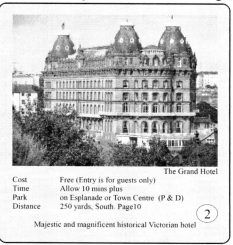

The Grand Hotel

Cost	Free (Entry is for guests only)
Time	Allow 10 mins plus
Park	on Esplanade or Town Centre (P & D)
Distance	250 yards, South. Page10

Majestic and magnificent historical Victorian hotel

(2)

When opened it was the largest and most handsome hotel in Europe and very little of the original outer structure has changed since that time. The interior would have been as grand if not grander than you would have expected of a hotel of such proportions and although greatly altered today you can still get the feeling of Victorian opulence when stepping inside. Guests visiting had the unusual option of hot or cold fresh or sea water baths, the sea water being pumped via a pipe directly from below.

In December 1914 during the bombardment of Scarborough the hotel took several hits and although the damage was small, times were changing and the hotel had reached and passed its zenith by this time.

During WW2 the hotel was used as a billet for RAF trainees and was eventually returned to its owners in a sad state of dilapidation. After several owners, in 1979 the hotel was purchased by Butlins and new life and investment were brought to the hotel. Although, some considered this a slip down market for such a fine building, the reality was Butlins maintained and improved the huge building with the associated costs that entails, whilst also bringing many thousands of visitors to the town.

The Grand was built on the site of Wood's lodging house, a favourite place to stay for Anne Bronte. Anne died from tuberculosis here and is buried in St. Mary's church graveyard on Scarborough's headland (see page 19).

Rare photograph show the Grand during construction

The Spa Bridge

On the 19th July 1827 the Cliff (Spa) Bridge was officially opened in front of an estimated ten thousand people and after the speeches, the procession traversed the bridge and followed the new walk down to the spa. Later in the evening a mail coach was driven at speed across the bridge with a sailor standing on the roof to prove the structure was strong enough for its intended passengers.

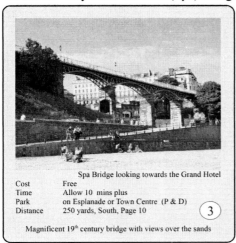

Spa Bridge looking towards the Grand Hotel

Cost   Free
Time   Allow 10 mins plus
Park   on Esplanade or Town Centre (P & D)
Distance   250 yards, South, Page 10   ③

Magnificent 19th century bridge with views over the sands

At a cost of just over seven thousand pounds the bridge had been built to enable easy and direct access from the town to the spa and was for some time the main entrance to the spa. Prior to this the cliff walk proved treacherous especially for the ladies in their fine dresses and the rather portly men that needed the facilities of the spa.

The charge for using the bridge was one penny and a further penny was charged should you require to take a glass of the waters. The bridge did not prove a financial success and despite many attempts to make it pay ownership eventually succumbed to the council who finally freed it from tolls and opened it to all in 1919.

Circa 1876

On the south end of the bridge can be found the Spa Chalet. Originally the home of the governor of the spa, this property has had many different uses since being redundant as the governors home, including private residence and at one time a cafe.

The Spa Bridge in its heyday of the early 1900's

The area beneath the bridge was at one time a major tourist area and host to an aquarium, a camera obscura and all manner of entertainments. These can be seen in the photograph to the left which shows this area in its heyday.

Scarborough Harbour

A visit to Scarborough Harbour and it's piers is a must for all visitors. During the day as well as an evening this area is generally humming with life.

The Sandside area (near the tourist information office) is currently undergoing major improvements and is gradually being transformed from the stereotypical seaside seafront into a more modern cultural area. The opening of quality eating houses in this area is already taking place and much needed improvements are commencing annually. Annoyingly, this has made finding a "kiss me quick" hat disappointingly difficult!

Scarborough harbour

Cost	Free (excludes, rides,amusements & chips)
Time	All Day
Park	Marine Drive , Town Centre (P & D) or Park and ride
Distance	Half mile, East, Page 10

(4)

Access to piers, lighthouse, amusements, boat trips, coffee houses and cafes. South bay beach, Lifeboat house, Ten pin bowling and Futurist theatre. Short walk to Spa entertainments and Marine drive around the castle headland.

On Sandside can be found "The ancient house of King Richard III". It is said that the King visited Scarborough in 1484 and took up temporary abode here. The house would originally have stood isolated and remains of mullioned windows opening on every side have been found. It is also believed that the house marks the shore position and that waves would have lapped up to these walls at that time.

Near the tourist information office can be found a rare glimpse of past times in the form of a police box. Police boxes were used in order for the police or public to contact the local police station using that very rare and expensive new invention, the telephone.

The harbour is still a working harbour and fishing boats can be seen unloading their catches on the west pier. In times gone by, so many fishing boats would be moored in the harbour it was said it was possible to walk across the harbour to the middle pier without touching the water.

All the piers are accessible on foot and the outer and middle piers are the most interesting for the casual visitor. From the middle pier (Old Pier) it is possible to access the lighthouse pier (Vincent's Pier). At the very end of Vincent's pier you will find a number seats to rest a while and absorb the sounds and smells of a typical seaside port.

For those of a stern stomach, you can take one of the pleasure boats that offer trips around the bay either at a gentle sedate pace or by screaming jet boat.

King Richard III house

The Scarborough Lifeboat

The Scarborough lifeboat has its current base at the start of the West Pier and it usually

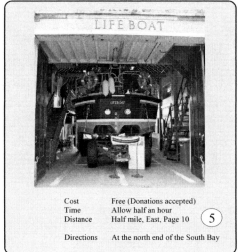

Cost	Free (Donations accepted)
Time	Allow half an hour
Distance	Half mile, East, Page 10
Directions	At the north end of the South Bay

(5)

possible to see the lifeboat sat in its house when the attached RNLI shop is open although access to the boat itself is not possible.

Scarborough has had a lifeboat since 1801. The original boat was built and supported by voluntary subscriptions at a cost of £152, she was 30 feet long and ten feet wide. At that time our seas were equivalent to the motorways of England now and carried vast amounts of traffic. A frightening number of these vessels came to grief, and, a great number of these were within close proximity to the shore. The need for lifeboats became a national requirement and in 1824 the RNLI was formed, albeit in a different name.

Many hundreds of lives have been saved by the various Scarborough lifeboats over the two hundred or so years and there are many tales of heroism and sad loss of life during that period, many lives being lost from the lifeboats themselves. An abridged report of one such tale is given below. Many more are available in book form.

28th October 1880. A storm of tremendous violence, of a strength not seen for 25 years, had arisen and vessels were dashing for the nearest port as quickly as they could. Twenty or more large vessels were making for Scarborough, only nine made it. Of those, only one was able to make fast to a pier and even that broke its moorings and was wrecked on the beach. The remaining eight were washed ashore and wrecked by the huge violent

surf, the lifeboat was in use throughout the day, and the following day, rowing back and forth through the surf saving sailors from a watery grave. During this storm not a life was lost in Scarborough's south bay, due entirely to the bravery and courage of the

The wreck of the Coupland, November 1861

lifeboatmen. Coxswain John Owston received a silver medal for his part in the rescue of twenty five lives during that storm. Tragically, many men perished further offshore.

St Mary's Church

Scarborough's oldest remaining church stands in a commanding position overlooking the old town on the headland just below the castle. Originally the site of a cistercian abbey, the present buildings date back to Norman times with many additions and destructions over the intervening years. A full history of the church can be found inside for those interested in more than the glancing facts provided here.

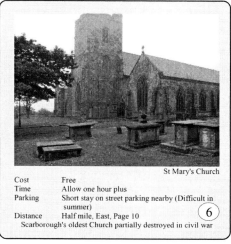

St Mary's Church

Prior to the civil war the church was a much larger building than remains today. In 1644 during one of the sieges of Scarborough Castle, roundhead, Sir John Meldrum took canon into the church and fired through the then east window pounding the castle with canon shot. The result was calamitous. The

Cost	Free
Time	Allow one hour plus
Parking	Short stay on street parking nearby (Difficult in summer)
Distance	Half mile, East, Page 10

(6)

Scarborough's oldest Church partially destroyed in civil war

besieged Royalists returned fire with no less than sixty pieces of ordnance shattering the fabric of the church bringing down the entire choir and north transept which were never rebuilt. The central tower was so badly damaged it fell down some 15 years later. The ruins are still visible in the churchyard.

In the graveyard across the road can be found the grave of Anne Bronte, of the famous literary family. Not a native of Scarborough, Anne came here many times during her life and loved the place so much she returned whilst trying to recover from the 'consumption'. She did not recover and died in Scarborough in May 1849 requesting to be buried here. After the gravestone had been erected, her sister Charlotte, on visiting the grave found five errors in the inscription and had to have them corrected. One error still remains, her age at death was 29 not 28.

After visiting the church take a wander down Mulgrave Place. Towards the end of the road is a building named "The castle by the Sea". This typically artisty house was the home for many years of the artist John Atkinson Grimshaw 1836-1893. Grimshaw is famous for his moody moonlit scenes of harbours, the sea, docks and all things maritime. Many of his paintings are of Scarborough and Whitby and fetch very high prices on the rare occasions these come up for auction. Several of his paintings are in Scarborough art gallery and well worth a visit. See page 20.

At the end of Mulgrave Place take a right turn and follow the 'secret' walk around the back of the castle by the sea towards the castle proper. Be careful as there is a steep drop and land slips occur here occasionally.

Anne Bronte's headstone

Scarborough Art Gallery

A small but significant collection works of art can be seen at the Art Gallery in The Crescent just off the Town Centre in Scarborough. A very modest charge for adults gains an entry ticket which is valid to the end of the year. On display is the permanent exhibition which has an interesting selection of local scenes and a temporary exhibition which will change throughout the year. There is a small cafe area and a resource room with children's activities, involving, as you might guess, drawing activities.

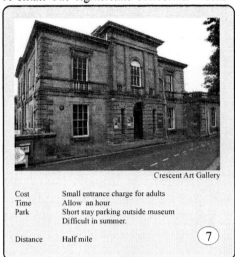
Crescent Art Gallery

Cost	Small entrance charge for adults
Time	Allow an hour
Park	Short stay parking outside museum Difficult in summer.
Distance	Half mile

(7)

The building was the first and the finest of the villas built on the south side of the crescent and was built around 1835 in an Italianate style. It has had various uses over the years, being at one time a maternity clinic before becoming the town's art gallery in 1947. The extensive cellars are now occupied by the arts workshop which also holds regular exhibitions.

The local scenes contain some stunning paintings by John Atkinson Grimshaw (1836-1893) who was a resident of Scarborough for many years in the "Castle by the sea" near St Mary's Church. Grimshaw is famous for his moody moonlit scenes of harbours, the sea, docks and all things maritime. Many of his paintings are of Scarborough and Whitby and fetch very high prices on the very rare occasions these come up for auction. Grimshaw's technique for producing such moonlit scenes is not clear, but it is known that he used photographs extensively and even tried painting over the top of photographs. Should you visit his "Castle by the sea" you may notice what is clearly a Victorian photographers window next to this building.

Scarborough can boast to be the birthplace of Frederick Leighton (1830-1896) the world acclaimed artist and president of the Royal Academy from 1878-1896. One of his many gargantuan classical works can be seen hanging on the stairway in the art gallery. In 1896 Leighton was given a peerage in the new year honours list, sadly, he died the following day making him Baron Leighton of Stretton for just one day.

Much of the collection housed within the art gallery (not all of the collection is actually on show) was bequeathed by the late Tom Laughton CBE who was a life long collector of fine art. Tom was the brother of actor Charles Laughton and a highly respected and successful hotelier in the town owning the towns Pavilion Hotel and the Royal Hotel. In fact, Tom collected and cataloged in his memoirs over three hundred major works of art in addition to hundreds of small oils, watercolours and prints that hung in the bedrooms and sitting rooms of the hotels. 68 of these works were gifted to Scarborough Corporation and a booklet is available free of charge illustrating half of these.

Peasholm Park

Peasholm park is a sparkling jewel in the crown of Scarborough's north bay area. The park first opened in 1912 and has been a popular place to relax and enjoy the simple pleasures of a park ever since. Recently it has undergone major improvements and this has enhanced the park considerably.

Parking is usually not too difficult on Peasholm drive to the south of the park, although, this is disc parking and limited to three hours. Parking to the north is outside the disc zone and not restricted. There are several pay and display car parks nearby.

The overall theme of the park is Japanese. There are pagodas, bandstands, bridges and ponds all in the same style. The park is centred on a large lake which hosts dragon shape boats for hire for a nominal charge. In

Dragon boats

Cost	Free. Charges for, boats, golf and occasionally for concerts or naval battles (summer season).
Park	P & D car park or free 2 hrs on street parking
Time	Allow 3 hours plus
Distance	Half mile, North West, Page 10
	Plenty of refreshments in the area (8)

the centre of the lake is an island which has a walkway around and up to the summit, where a newly formed Japanese garden can be seen with bridges, water features and seating areas. Whilst walking round the island you will also see the miniature ships which are used in a naval battle reconstruction which takes place on various days during the week. Usually there is a charge to enter the area during the battles.

Exploring further you will find paths, ponds, waterfalls, cascades and a multitude of other attractions in the park. There are sculptures and wildlife, particularly squirrels, which are very tame. It is possible to feed them from your hand, much to the delight of children. The park is always buzzing with life and is kept in tip top condition by the council park keepers.

An 18 hole mini golf course is very popular and a round can be enjoyed for a small charge per person, depending on how many balls you lose! And, don't try to convince the green keeper a squirrel made off with your ball, he has heard that one all too often!

It is easy to spend a whole morning here and it is best to take a picnic. Once exhausted, cross the road and find the Scarborough miniature railway.

Japanese garden

Scarborough Spa

Scarborough spa is the first and oldest of Scarborough's tourist attractions. The history of Scarborough tourism is based on this spot. For the exact spot you need to stand on the mini roundabout in front of the north end of the spa. Under here lies the original spa well used by generations of fine ladies and gentlemen that frequented the spa in times gone by. They would come in order to consume the cleansing and therapeutic waters which had gained a reputation for their health giving properties.

The Spa

Cost	Free, Park on Esplanade
Time	Allow 30 mins plus
Distance	less than 1 mile, South, Page 10

(9)

If you take the steps down to the sands from here you will still find the spa waters flowing from a small spout in the sea wall. This is the Townspeoples well and was provided for local people at a time when charges for taking the waters were introduced. Scarborough people upon finding they were being charged for the waters made great protestations, and the company running the spa provided this well to enable them to continue with their right to free water. It is not advisable to try drinking this water as recent chemical analysis proved it to be less than pure.

There have been several different buildings at the Spa most of which have come to some sort of sticky end. One set of buildings were destroyed by an "earthquake" which also sealed up the spa waters for a short time. The building prior to the one standing now was completely destroyed by fire in September 1876 with the present buildings being erected a short time after.

Aside from taking the waters, visitors would be treated to music and dance and other forms of entertainment in the spa buildings. A full programme of military and brass bands, singers, illusionists and the like would keep visitors returning on a daily basis.

The Spa circa 1920

Eventually, the original water taking purpose of the spa disappeared leaving the grand entertainment buildings we now see. Currently the spa hosts many different functions, conferences and events and lately even weddings, but, you can still wander around the magnificent old building and admire the fine detail of the mid Victorian architecture.

Scarborough South Cliff

A tour of Scarborough's Victorian south Cliff. Cast your imagination back a hundred years to a time where things happened slower and time was apparently more relaxed.

Queen Victoria is on the throne and that new invention the steam locomotive has brought you to this prosperous and vibrant resort by the sea. New lodging houses towering over the cliff side have just been built, some even, have electricity.

On a Sunday morning after visiting church in their finest clothes Churchgoers would parade along the South Cliff meeting and greeting as they sauntered slowly along.

The whole width of the Esplanade would be taken up with the mass of people taking part in this "Church Parade". Ladies carrying parasols and fans would gently bow their heads as gentlemen casually doff their hats. Children run in and out of the crowds and horses splutter as they try to pull their carriage as they fight their way through the crowd. The photograph below captures this regular promenade in action.

South cliff gardens

Cost	Free
Time	Allow one hour plus
	On street parking
Distance	Less than 1 mile, South, Page 10

(10)

Of course, times have changed, but along Scarborough's South Cliff it is still possible, with a little imagination, to envisage what must have been such delightful sights on a Sunday morning.

Parking on the road somewhere near where The Esplanade meets Holbeck Hill is free and it is usually easy to find a space. Take a walk starting at The Clock Tower and using the following entries as your guide along the way. Allow around two hours to complete this tour at a very leisurely pace.

The Clock Tower (p24)
The Star Disk (p25)
The Spa (p22)
The South Cliff Lift (p26)

Church Parade circa 1890

23

The Clock Tower

The visitor may be more familiar with this area than at first realised, as, in recent years the

The Clock Tower

Cost	Free – park on Esplanade
Time	Allow 30 mins plus
Distance	Less than 1 mile, South, Page 10

(11)

area around the clock tower has been used as the outside setting for the hospital television series 'The Royal' set in the 1960's. If you are lucky you may witness filming taking place and see how the natural beauty of the area is used as a backdrop.

The Clock Tower was presented to the town by Alfred Shuttleworth in 1911 and was probably designed by Frank Tugwell who was also the architect for Red Court and also parts of The Spa. Red Court is the building on the opposite side of the road and was built in 1900 as a private house. It has never been a hospital except in dramatic recreations.

On the opposite side of the road is a hidden public garden, also, with Mr Shuttleworth as benefactor. It is poorly maintained at the present, but, it originally was a garden to stimulate the senses and contained plants that exhibited wonderful aromas. To enable blind and partially sighted visitors to enjoy the garden all the plants had name plaques written in braille.

This part of the Esplanade was the wealthiest part of Scarborough in Victorian times and all the houses now converted to flats would have been individual homes. If you wander along the footpath towards the town you will come across some pieces of glass set into the pavement. This is a roof light for an old tunnel constructed under the road to enable the original owner of the house opposite, George Lord Beeforth, Mayor of Scarborough in early 1900's, to access his garden under the Esplanade carriage road. The name of the garden in those times was the Belvedere Rose Garden, and, was quite a grand affair judging by the descriptions found in old books. During one bazaar held in the garden an elephant was brought as an attraction. It would seem the Elephant came to no harm amongst the roses, but, the grounds were not improved by the visit! It is still just possible amongst the undergrowth to make out the now unused exit arch. The rose gardens still exist and are now cared for by the parks department of Scarborough Council who continue to make great efforts to keep this area in pristine condition.

Down from the clock tower can be found the old bowling green, now used as a putting green in summer. Spend a few pounds to hire a club and try your hand whilst over looking the Scarborough harbour and headland one of the finest views in the area.

A maze of beautifully tended public gardens can be found in the area from the clock tower down towards the sea and spa complex.

The Star Disk

A fascinating piece of work, and, the largest illuminated star disk in the United Kingdom.
The disk is 26m across and has 42 sunken lights representing the brightest stars in the northern skies.   It is possible to make out The Plough,Cassiopeia, The Little Bear, and Draco the Dragon.

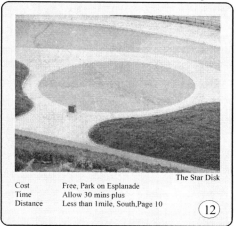

There are marks for various dates during the year and if you stand on these marks and look directly north (St Mary's Church is directly north) at midnight on that particular date then the star disk will mirror the stars in the sky.

It is also possible to see the position of sunrise on various dates by standing in the centre of the disk and look towards the marks on the inner wall seat.   According to the instructions, midnight on the 21st June is the optimal viewing date.

The Star Disk

Cost	Free, Park on Esplanade
Time	Allow 30 mins plus
Distance	Less than 1mile, South,Page 10

(12)

The site on which the star disk is constructed was originally a grand outdoor sea water

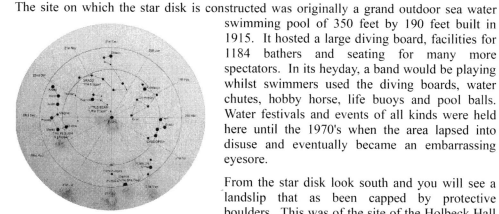

swimming pool of 350 feet by 190 feet built in 1915. It hosted a large diving board, facilities for 1184 bathers and seating for many more spectators. In its heyday, a band would be playing whilst swimmers used the diving boards, water chutes, hobby horse, life buoys and pool balls. Water festivals and events of all kinds were held here until the 1970's when the area lapsed into disuse and eventually became an embarrassing eyesore.

From the star disk look south and you will see a landslip that as been capped by protective boulders. This was of the site of the Holbeck Hall Hotel, the hotel that "fell into the sea" in 1993 a victim of coastal erosion.

The South Bay Swimming Pool, Circa 1920

The South Cliff Lift

Opened in 1875 it is believed the south cliff lift was one of, if not the, first hydraulic funicular railway to be built in Great Britain. It was built specifically to transport passengers from the Spa to the hotels and boarding houses on the Esplanade.

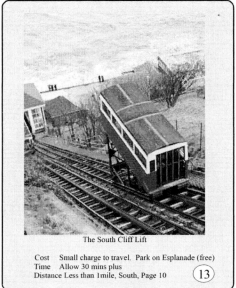

The South Cliff Lift

Cost   Small charge to travel. Park on Esplanade (free)
Time   Allow 30 mins plus
Distance Less than 1mile, South, Page 10   (13)

A water counterbalancing method was used to work the railway. Each of the two carriages had a water tank under the carriage floor and the top most carriage was filled with water until its weight exceeded the lower carriage and then the brake was released. When the heavy carriage reached the bottom, the water was emptied and pumped back up to the top station using two gas, and later, steam pumps. This method is no longer in use as the whole system was modernised in 1997.

Currently, little is made of the importance of this lift. It is presently kept in excellent order by Scarborough Council and it would be sad if it were to follow the path of other funiculars in the town that have ended up scrapped or sold to other towns. Take the time to visit this important piece of British history whilst it is still accessible and working.

A trip on the lift from the Spa is highly recommended, especially if you have parked your car on the Esplanade as the walk up the cliff can be very tiresome after a hot day on the beach.

View of the cliff lift in the late 1800's

Oliver's Mount

Oliver's Mount is the site of Scarborough's main War Memorial as well as being a major motorcycle road racing track.

There is not a great deal to visit here, but, is included because of the magnificent views over the town of that can be seen from the War Memorial and it is worth a visit just for those alone.

Oliver's Mount was named after the mistaken belief that Cromwell erected batteries here against Scarborough castle, during the siege of the castle in 1644-5. Indeed, there is no evidence that Cromwell ever visited Scarborough at all.

War memorial at Oliver's Mount

Cost	Free
Time	Allow 20 mins plus
Park	On road or car park (free)
Distance	1.5 miles, South, Page 10

(14)

Dramatic views across Scarborough and the coast line from this high viewpoint.

The road racing track is still used on two or three times a year to host motorcycles races and a festival of speed at weekends in May, June and September.

The war memorial was unveiled in 1923 and paid for by public subscription of around £5000.

Included on the memorial are the names of the 17 civilians killed as a result of the seaborne bombardment on December 16th 1914. The first British civilian casualties of World War One came as a result of three German battleships pounding the town with over 500 shells hitting over 200 hundred properties and injuring a further 84 people over a period of half an hour during the early morning. If you happen to visit The Crescent or Art Gallery during your visit to Scarborough, you will notice the outside walls are pock marked. These are the shrapnel marks from this shelling and are startling reminders of this tragic attack.

A shell passed through the tower of the lighthouse after ricocheting off The Grand Hotel, later the tower had to be demolished. Surprisingly, the lighthouse wasn't rebuilt until the 1930's.

During the raid mines were laid along the coast in an indiscriminate attempt to disable shipping off the East Coast. These mines proved to be deadly over a long period and were still being caught in the nets of fishing trawlers right up to the 1970's. One of these, now defused, mines can still be seen displayed on Sandside near the foreshore at Scarborough.

The Mere

As recent as twenty five years ago this natural stretch of water was buzzing with life and

The Mere

Cost	Free
Time	Allow one to two hours
Equipment	Bread for ducks
Distance	2 miles, South West, Page 10

(15)

Tranquil lake near town centre. Picnic and fishing location

vitality. During that period The Mere was used as a tourist attraction featuring rowing boats, paddle boats, golf putting, fishing, carefully tended gardens, a cafe and a pirate ship named "The Hispaniola" which took small children onto the island to search for doubloons! (This boat now offers trips from Scarborough harbour) All these attractions have now gone and the area is slowly reverting back to the wildlife area it once was.

Good fishing is still possible and day tickets are available at modest cost and there is excellent disabled access. Contact Scarborough tourist information office for further details.

Situated on the southern outskirts of Scarborough in the shadow of Olivers Mount (see page 27), now, the area is abundant with wildlife and a walk around the lake is enjoyed by many locals and visitors alike. Children love feeding the ducks and a healthy colony of Canadian Geese make this their home when in the country. Parking is easy and plentiful and there are picnic tables on what was once the putting green. Towards the southern end is a little known about children's play area.

Just to show that although currently in a state of change, this area has been the subject of change on previous occasions and below is an extract from Theakston's Guide to Scarborough dated 1853. *"Formerly a fine sheet of water, abounding with pike, perch, and eels; but recently much contracted by the formation of the railroad which runs on one side. The growth of vegetation, and the deposit of sediment which has been accumulating for years, have also materially aided in converting the lake on whose bosom the majestic swan was wont to repose, into a shallow and useless marsh. It once afforded excellent diversion to the angler; but, except when the frosts of winter congeal its surface, causing it to become a scene of animation, it possesses no attraction beyond the pleasant walk along its margin in returning from a summer day's ramble in the neighbourhood."*

A view of The Mere in the 1930's

Scarborough to Whitby Railway

Trains no longer run on the Scarborough to Whitby line as it was closed and dismantled as a result of the Beeching cuts in the 1960's. Since then it has gained a new lease of life as a public footpath and cycleway and is used by hundreds of walkers and riders everyday. Ironically, probably more traffic uses the line today than did when it closed to locomotives in the sixties.

Scenic and without any steep gradients it is an ideal place for an outing for those looking for a less challenging walk or cycle. The section most worthy of a visit is the 10 mile section from Cloughton through Ravenscar to Robin Hoods Bay.

Scarborough to Whitby pathway

Cost	Free
Time	Allow 4 hrs
Directions	Starts at Cloughton 4ml north of Scarborough
Equipment	OS map OL27,bikes, boots, etc.
Distance	4 miles +, North west, Page 10

(16)

On road parking can be found at most intersections with the minor roads that pass under or over the line. Parking at the Hayburn Wyke Hotel is possible, although this is for customers only, which is not too difficult a task to accomplish by use of their public bar!

Halfway along the route, at Ravenscar, the line detours onto the minor roads due to a tunnel. There is plenty of parking at Ravenscar, which is worth a visit in itself. (see page 44) The line gently climbs in both directions towards Ravenscar. North of Ravenscar the line cuts through the old alum mines now owned by the National Trust, but once a huge concern extracting Alum for use in the dyeing process.

Further north the line is again blocked and the path deviates through quaint cliff side village of Robin Hoods Bay (see page 47) and continues at the northern side towards Whitby.

The track is also part of the Moors to Sea long distance cycle route which cover eighty miles inland to Pickering.

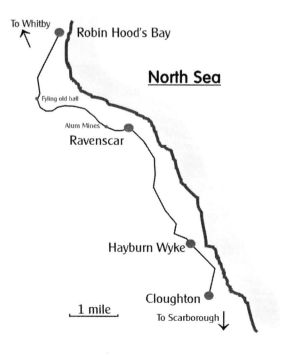

To Whitby

Robin Hood's Bay

North Sea

Fyling old hall

Alum Mines

Ravenscar

Hayburn Wyke

Cloughton

1 mile

To Scarborough

Walking with the dinosaurs

In a bay just north of Scarborough can be found a wealth of evidence of prehistoric

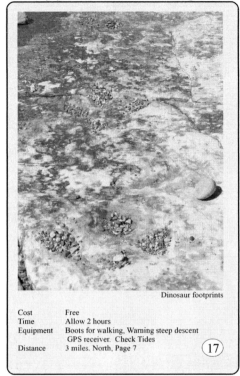

dinosaurs in the form of footprints in rock. Recognising dinosaur footprints is not easy and even experts don't always identify these correctly. However, if you follow the instructions below, for which you need a GPS receiver, not only will you find a string several large footprints but you will also be treated to some very interesting rock formations en route.

A GPS receiver is required, because without guidance it is virtually impossible to spot these foot prints, even when stood on top of them.

Access to the location is a little difficult and is not suitable for pushchairs, wheelchairs, disabled persons or, indeed, the faint of heart. Children will love it! There is a walk of around 1.25 miles from the nearest parking. The walking will be difficult and treacherous in bad or wet weather. **Please check the tides before setting out.** The footprints are fairly close to the shore but are covered at high tide.

Dinosaur footprints

Cost	Free
Time	Allow 2 hours
Equipment	Boots for walking, Warning steep descent GPS receiver. Check Tides
Distance	3 miles. North, Page 7

(17)

The nearest free on street parking is at the top of Scalby Mills (N54° **18.077** W0° **24.800**) or if you wish to pay to save a few yards legwork you can park outside the Sea Life Centre. Head towards and cross the footbridge at Scalby Mills Hotel (N54° **18.168** W0° **24.588**) continue up the bank at the other side and follow the sign for the Cleveland Way. Follow the main footpath up and along to N54° **18.358** W0° **24.802**. At this point follow the narrow

track/path directly down the cliff towards the concrete sewer pipe. Proceed directly to N 54° **18.793** W 000° **25.100**

You are looking for a series of about six footprints in the stone, each footprint is around 1 metre from the next. They are not clearly defined as they have been eroded by the sea, and you may struggle to see them. However, once you have located one, the others will become obvious. The footprints have three forward facing claws and a smaller back claw.

Dinosaur footprint indentions

Note: After heavy seas these footprints can be covered with shingle and subsequently be difficult to locate.

Forge Valley

Situated 4 miles to the west of Scarborough town can be found Forge Valley. The valley was created by glacial melt waters in the last ice age and is now a site of special scientific interest (SSSI). This densely wooded valley can be accessed from either end via the village of Ayton in the south or from the Throxenby area of Scarborough to the east. Free parking is possible at several locations through the valley, with the two largest areas being near "Old mans mouth" petrifying spring, which is a suggested starting point to explore the valley.

Forge Valley

Cost	Free
Time	Allow two to three hours
Equipment	Strong footwear, OSOL27 Map
Distance	4.5 Miles, West, Page 7

Scenic walking along the river Derwent   (18)

Forge Valley has been visited by tourists since early Victorian times due to its close proximity to the town of Scarborough and the wealth of wildlife the valley contains. Indeed sightings of Woodpeckers and Kingfishers are quite common by the river. The name of the valley is due to the fact that a forge and iron foundry were situated here, opposite the "Old mans mouth", up until the early 1800's. The river Derwent meanders its way lazily through the full length of the valley on its way through Ayton and inland towards Malton and beyond.

There are several paths along the length of the valley. On the west side of the river a boarded walkway follows the edge of the river towards Ayton, and, although the boardway stops short of the village itself it is possible to continue on the public footpath to village passing Ayton Castle enroute. The 14th century castle was once a very grand and large affair with the buildings extending to more than acre, but now neglected and returning to nature.

On the east side of the valley there is a criss cross of paths through the dense woodland and disused quarries which are a rich source of fossils. Boards have been erected at various locations explaining the area in more detail. There is a waymarked geological trail starting at the 'Old mans mouth' car park which covers approximately 3 miles and should take 2-3 hours. Some

The forge circa 1798

of the paths are steep and sturdy footwear is advisable. A leaflet is available from Scarborough tourist information centre explaining this route in considerable detail.

31

The Cloughton Stone Circle

To the eye not much to view but worth a visit if the reader has any interest in antiquity and half an hour or so to spare.

Part of the stone circle

Cost	Free
Time	Allow half an hour
Equipment	Tracks to the circle can be very muddy
Distance	7 Miles, North West, Page 6

(19)

Little known about well preserved stone circle.

It is usually possible park at the track gate (dotted line on the map) on the main road, or, failing that there is plenty of parking near the Falcon Inn.

The circle lies on private land adjacent to the Forestry Commission's Harwood Dale forest therefore it is possible to view the circle without encroaching on private land. There is no public footpath, however the forestry commission allow access for walkers onto their property. There is a good track from the main A171 Scarborough to Whitby road, this deteriorates into a muddy sometimes impassable quagmire as you near the circle.

The track from the road follows a very ancient boundary that splits the forest of Pickering with the Abbot of Whitby lands. This border was marked by boundary stones and four of these are still marked on the current 1:25,000 ordnance survey map, two before reaching the circle and two a short way after. It may still be possible to identify these stones.

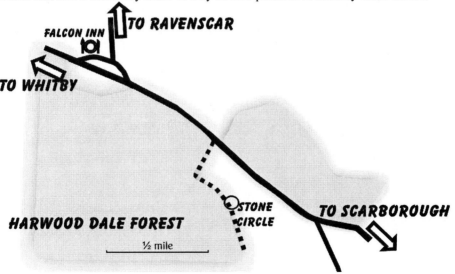

Research has gleaned virtually nothing about this ancient monument,indeed, The Rev. A.N. Cooper in his book "The curiosities of East Yorkshire" devotes an entire extended chapter to the circle, but, fails to reveal any single fact and wanders off into the realms of speculative stories of druids and marriage rites.

Filey Country Park

Filey Country Park is an ideal spot to while away a day as there is just so much to do around this area. Park-up in the country park at the far end nearest the brigg. In this area there are superb views across the sands towards Flamborough Head and the quaint old town of Filey to enjoy whilst eating your sandwiches,

Use this car park as a base to visit the sands, brigg & town. If you arrange your visit to coincide with a low tide you will be able to walk all the way along the Filey Brigg promontory (page 34) and out into the North Sea on your way witnessing a huge array of seashore wildlife. Children can spend hours in the rock pools searching for crabs and other horrible squirmy things.

The Wolds Way Meets The Cleveland Way

Cost	Pay & Display parking charge (Apr to Oct)
Time	Allow all day
Distance	7 miles, South East, Page 11

(20)

Directions
Follow signs for Filey Town centre until you pick up the signs for the Country Park. Easy to find.

The park has two children's play areas and a huge grassed area suitable for ball games or the flying of kites and the like. Access to the beach is via the pathway at the centre of the park opposite the cafe.

The long distance paths, The Cleveland Way and The Wolds way both terminate on the top of Carr Naze (the grassed area above the Brigg). If you fancy, you can walk north towards Scarborough along the Cleveland Way for a while along the top of dramatic cliffs eroded by the force of the North Sea over the mists of time.

In the opposite direction it is possible to walk towards St Oswald's Church and visit the graveyard to see just how many fishermen died out at sea in times gone by. Here you will soon appreciate just how dangerous the life of a fisherman used to be. (See page 36)

Take the ravine bridge near the church and head into the town of Filey. If you take the first (road) left after the bridge you will find the small Filey museum on your right. (see page 35) This small but well maintained museum is worth a visit if you can find the time.

Finally, a walk along Filey promenade and an ice cream or a game of crazy golf and some soggy chips and you will have filled a whole day here.

View along Filey Brigg towards Flamborough

Filey Brigg

The Devils Tongue and Philaw-Bridge are just two of the names given in past times to this

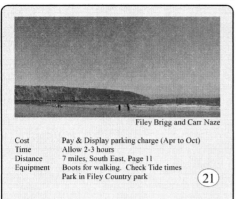

Filey Brigg and Carr Naze

Cost	Pay & Display parking charge (Apr to Oct)
Time	Allow 2-3 hours
Distance	7 miles, South East, Page 11
Equipment	Boots for walking. Check Tide times
	Park in Filey Country park (21)

spit of land extending around half a mile into the North Sea. There is no doubt that without this geological oddity the town of Filey would never have existed. Protecting the area from the ravages of the north wind gales that batter this coast the brigg is gradually being eroded and soon access along the top will be gone with the wind.

Access to the Brigg is best made via Filey Country Park (see page 33). Filey Brigg is best visited at low tide and care should be taken when visiting from the beach that the tide does not cut off your return route.

A leaflet is available from Filey tourist information office (Located in Filey Town Centre) that describes in considerable detail the geology and history of the brigg.

The upper grassed area now virtually eroded away is called Carr Naze. This was considerably larger in Roman times and was used as a base for a signal station to warn locals of any sea borne invaders. Walk along Carr Naze and you will appreciate just why they chose this spot, as, to the north Scarborough is clearly visible, to the south Flamborough, whilst inland, the ridge of the Wolds is within easy view. The stone bases for the signal station are now situated in the town gardens. On the north side at the base of the cliff a large natural ampitheatre can be seen, this is know locally as The Emperors Bath, supposedly used by the Roman Emperor Constantine or Severus during one of their visits, but more probably a romantic Victorian notion.

A walk along the base of the Brigg brings a completely different set of delights. The path

1920's Angler on Filey Brigg

along the base of the brigg takes you well out into the North Sea and enroute you will witness a multitude of bird life and if lucky you may even spot a seal amongst the rocks. Rock pools will entertain adults and children alike with a vast array of colourful seaweeds, crabs, anemones and the like.

At very low tide towards the end of the Brigg can be seen a second promontory pointing out towards Flamborough, this is named 'The Spittals' and current thinking, although yet to be proved, is that this is the remains of a Roman Harbour. It is possible for a short period at very low tide, with sturdy footwear and a steadying stick, to venture onto 'The Spittals' and make your own romantic conclusions.

Filey Museum

Run entirely by volunteers and housed in two preserved historic cottages this museum traces the history of Filey over many generations. This is a small museum and is reflected in the modest entrance fee.

The museum buildings date from the 17th century, one having been a fisherman's cottage and the other a farm cottage. The buildings were saved from demolition in the late 1960s and first opened to the public as a local history museum in 1971. The museum is kept updated and well maintained and in 2006 won a small visitor attraction award.

Filey Museum

Cost	Small charge per person
Time	Allow 1 hour plus
Access	11:00-17:00, Sat 14:00-1700
Distance	7 miles, South East, Page 11
Directions	Park in Filey Country Park or Town
	Open in summer season (April-October)

(22)

The exhibits bring to life the history of Filey and it's inextricable link with the sea through birth, life and death.

Displays show things as diverse as lifeboats and their crew to fine Victorian visitors and their pastimes. There is fascinating section on Fishermen's jumpers or Ganseys as they are called. In the past each community on the East Coast had their own style of knitting a Gansey and it was possible to tell where someone was from by looking at their jumper. Apparently this came in useful when dead bodies were washed ashore after a tragedy at sea.

The museum is usually manned by older members of the community who love to answer questions, which in turn means it is often a struggle to get away from the museum once entrapped.

An interesting section on fossils and rocks of the area should keep young minds lively. Whilst older members might be more attracted to reading the copies of old newspapers on display which give a fascinating insight into Victorian society. One of the primary functions of these early newspapers was

Filey sea wall

to list all those visiting the town thus enabling visitors and locals to be aware of the nobility in the area at any given time.

St Oswald's Church, Filey

This guide does not intend to go into great detail on the history of St Oswald's church as
there are other volumes dedicated to this and they tend to require serious concentration to absorb the vast and occasionally questionable facts. Suffice to say, the Church is worth a visit and the one or two notes below might give the visitor a reason to ponder and stay a while.

St. Oswald's Church

Cost	Donations accepted
Time	Allow 30 mins plus
Equipment	Boots for walking
Distance	7 miles, South East, Page 11

(23)

Park in Filey Country Park, Town Centre or Church Ravine
(free)

It is not known why the church was built on this site, as, the valley named Church Ravine isolates the church from the town, and, although this ravine is now easy to cross, in times gone by, there would have been a rapid stream flowing and no bridge to cross it.

Some historians speculate that the original town of Filey was centred on the area now know as the Country Park . This holds some
credibility given the location of the Roman signal station on Carr Naze and entertains the possibility that the original church was constructed from materials plundered from the station.

The ravine marks the boundary of the North and East Ridings of Yorkshire and gives rise to a local saying. When referring to the final journey to the churchyard it was described as "He's gaing acrass ti' North".

Graveyards can be difficult places to consider visiting, but in St Oswald's case take the effort to wander through a few of the headstones and see just how many men have been

St Oswald's circa 1820

taken whilst out at sea . Imagine the number of times the hymn "For those in peril upon the sea...." must have been sung at this church.

An unusual feature is the shape of the weather "cock" on top of the spire.

From 1880 to 1935 the Vicar of Filey was the Rev. A.N. Cooper. A truly remarkable man who wrote numerous history books
and tales of his travels walking across Europe. He was known as "The Walking Parson" and was highly liked and respected by all who met him.

The Filey Lifeboat

Filey has always supported a small but effective fishing fleet, although, currently this has dwindled to a state where the use of the word fleet is perhaps a little over enthusiastic. The Lifeboat at Filey has always been inextricably linked with the fishing community with most of the crew being drawn from this brave sea hardy stock. The signal for the launching of the Filey lifeboat was until recently an explosive maroon which was fired high into the sky by a rocket where it explodes with a reverberating crash disturbing thousands of seabirds who squawk in a chorus of annoyance. For anyone in trouble out on the water in Filey Bay this is one of the sweetest sounds they were likely to hear in their entire lifetime.

Filey Lifeboat

Cost	No charges
Time	Allow half an hour
Distance	7 miles, South East, Page 11

(24)

Access to the lifeboat house is restricted and not available to the public. However, a visit to the Cobble Landing and seafront is recommended.

There is a small RNLI shop at the lifeboat house which is situated on the Cobble Landing, however, access to the boats is restricted. Just opposite the life boat house can usually be found the brightly painted Cobbles. Cobbles in this sense meaning the clinker built boats of a design used for hundreds of years by the local fishermen. The lifeboat house has a small shop where it is possible to buy a copy of the Story of the Filey Lifeboats which lists the courage and tragedies that have befallen the lifeboat over the past two hundred years. There are currently two lifeboats, the larger boat is used for offshore operations or where the smaller inshore inflatable boat is unable to operate.

Filey Dams Nature Reserve

Very much a hidden gem, this six hectare nature reserve can be found hiding behind the

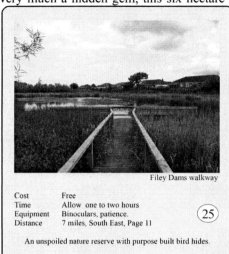

Filey Dams walkway

Cost	Free
Time	Allow one to two hours
Equipment	Binoculars, patience.
Distance	7 miles, South East, Page 11

(25)

An unspoiled nature reserve with purpose built bird hides.

modern Wharfedale housing estate off the main Filey to Bridlington road on the outskirts of Filey.   There is a small free parking area near the entrance and parking is not generally a problem.   Access is free but is restricted to the walkways and bird hides only.   There are two hides, main hide and east hide, each with seating and lift up viewing flaps.

The reserve is very much a nature enthusiasts area rather than a casual visitors venue and children might find the experience a little tedious.   It is essential to have the correct equipment, as, you will be considered naked if you are not wearing a good set of binoculars.   The area consists of three separate lakes, marsh and neutral land shared by farm stock.   It is essential to pick the right weather to visit here and also to allow plenty of time to watch the numerous forms of wildlife.

Depending on the time of year visited it is possible to see rich insect and bird life and occasional large mammals, such as, fox and deer.   It is an important resting place for migrant wading birds and wildfowl.   Insects include butterflies and a considerable number of different species of dragonflies.   Many different types of reed and water borne plants cover the marsh and edges of the lakes.

View from main hide

For those interested in bird watching there are two other places where multitudes of different breeds of birds can be seen in this area.   Closest by is Filey Brigg where huge quantities of seabirds can be seen feeding on the sands and rocks of the Brigg.   (See page 34)   Another place of national importance is the 300ft high chalk cliffs at Bempton RSPB reserve (see page 51).   This reserve can be found 7 mile south east.

Dalby Forest

There are a multitude of things to do in Dalby Forest, so much in fact, that several of the activities have a page devoted to them alone. Dalby forest is accessed via the nine mile toll road, Dalby Forest Drive, from either Langdale End or Thornton Le Dale at opposite ends. The most sceneic route to access the start of the drive is to take the back roads through Forge Valley near Ayton and through Langdale End.

The Adderstone, Dalby forest

Cost	Toll road. Charge per car per day. Discounted weekly ticket available.	
Time	All day	
Access	Via Langdale End or Thornton le Dale	26
Distance	7 ½ miles, West, Page 6	

At first sight the road toll can appear quite expensive but this should not put visitors off as it is quite easy to stay a full day in this forest, indeed, you will probably find several days worth of outside activities here.

To start your visit it is best to park near the new visitor centre near Low Dalby to obtain information on the vast array of walks, cycle tracks, play and barbecue areas and attractions accessible from the forest. Here you will also find a cafe and an education suite. There are disabled access walks as well as tree top climbing using the Go Ape site (extra payment required).

Particularly well catered for in this forest are cyclists, with easy, medium and hard off road routes as well as a huge stunt area, all free to access. If you haven't taken your own bikes, then bike hire is available at Low Dalby. At Low Dalby, in the village, the courtyard area has picnic tables, craft units and a cafe.

Dalby pages ;

Cycling in Dalby Forest - p40
The Bridestones - p41
Walking in Dalby Forest & Blakey Topping - p42

Sculptures in Dalby forest

There are many areas to park a car in the forest, the two most popular being Low Dalby, near the visitor centre and Adderstone field. Both of these have children's play areas. Quieter and more secluded areas are Crosscliff and Bickley.

Cycling in Dalby Forest

The thrill of off road cycling is a pleasure all adults and children should partake of at sometime in their life, and, Dalby forest is one of the best areas in the country to take advantage of this popular sport.

It goes without saying, that (at the least) helmets should be worn at all times. The trees are hard and the ground harder, and, both are met with more regularly than anticipated. Also, from personal experience, take an OS map, water, mobile phone (not all areas accessible), toolkit and ideally a gps receiver.

Off road cycle track, Dalby foreste

Cost	Toll road. Charge per car per day. Discounted weekly ticket available.
Time	All day
Access	Via Langdale End or Thornton le Dale
Distance	7 ½ miles, West, Page 6

(27)

Details of the waymarked routes are available from the visitor centre. A good starting point is Adderstone field, where you can pick up all four of the major circular waymarked routes, in order of difficulty, Green, Blue, Red and Black. Follow any one of these and you will be taken deep into the forest teeming with wildlife and vegetation. Amongst the multitude of animals wild deer can often be seen grazing.

Opposite Adderstone field is Dixons Hollow. Dixons Hollow is three acres of disused quarry that has been turned into an impressive free ride cycle skills park. Beams, jumps, see saws, bridges, berms, tabletops and skinnies.

Cycle and equipment hire is available at the village of Low Dalby near the visitor centre.

The Moors to Sea cycle route passes through Dalby forest.

This complex eighty mile route connects Whitby in the north with Scarborough in the south and as far inland as Pickering on predominantly off road or quiet lane routes.

Dixons Hollow

The Bridestones

There are many strange tales written about how these large naturally eroded rocks acquired their name. One of which, suggests, that in times gone by running races were an important part of a village wedding celebrations, and, after a wedding on the moors it was the custom for the newly married couple to be pursued at some pace towards the Bridestones by the villagers after having been given a few minutes start.

Almost all of the ancient wedding customs have been long forgotten and subsequently it is impossible know the exact reason for their naming, suffice to say, there are quite a number of similarly named "Bridestones" to be found throughout the country.

One of the Bridestones

Cost	Toll road. Charge per car per day. Discounted weekly ticket available.
Time	All day
Access	Via Langdale End or Thornton le Dale Park in Staindale Car Park
Distance	7 ½ miles, West, Page 6

(28)

Access to the Bridestones is easiest from the Staindale car park on the Dalby Forest drive. A two mile circular walk, some uphill, takes visitors through the forest and on to these amazing Jurassic rock formations formed as a result of millions of years of air and water erosion.

The area is now owned and preserved as a nature reserve by the National Trust and contains considerable wildlife. The path takes visitors through a mixture of ancient woodlands thought to date back to the last ice age and heather topped moors.

Children particularly like this walk as they usually enjoy clambering over the huge weathered rocks and exploring the hidden caves. You will see many parents grimace as they watch their offspring in horror fearlessly bounding around the over-hanging ledges.

In foggy conditions keep to the main paths as it is very easy to get disorientated on these moors.

Bridestones

41

Walking in Dalby Forest

A walkers paradise. A visit to the new visitor centre at Low Dalby is essential as here you

will find vast amounts of information on all the different grades of waymarked walking trails in the forest together with details of longer distance walking, maps and so on.

Dalby forest encompasses a vast area which includes lowland woods, streams, valleys, arable farmland all the way up to bleak heather covered moorland, so, there are walks of all types and ease of access, including one with wheelchair or buggy access.

It is possible to tie in a walk with use of the Moorsbus service to enable non circular routes to be made, although, careful planning will be required for this.

Cost	Toll road. Charge per car per day. Discounted weekly ticket available.
Time	All day
Access	Via Langdale End or Thornton le Dale
Distance	7 ½ miles, West, Page 6

(29)

This book does not include any details of specific walks as it is beyond its scope, however, as a rough guide, we suggest the Bickley Forest waymarked trail for an easy and wheelchair access walk. Parking in the Bridestones car park gives access to The Bridestones circular trail which makes for a longer, slightly more strenuous and very rewarding circular walk. This area is now owned and maintained by the National Trust.

Finally for the more adventurous, parking at Crosscliffe car park it is possible to see,

Bridestones walk

from the viewing point, the unmistakable hump of Blakey Topping to the north west. This natural mini mountain is approximately two miles from the view point and makes for a not too strenuous four mile return walk. The area is now owned by the National Trust and must have been a religious site in distant yores as a close inspection reveals a stone circle and various standing stones nearby.

The best mapping for this and the surrounding area is the Ordnance Survey OL27 leisure map which can be obtained from most local stores. Weather conditions in this area can change and deteriorate rapidly and it wise to take equipment suitable for navigating in rain or fog . It should also be noted that mobile phone coverage is not good in some parts of the forest and its surrounding area.

St Margaret's Chapel, Harwood Dale

Churches can be quite surprising places to visit, what on the outside looks like a standard run-of-the-mill affair can often hide a fascinating array of facts and history. St Margarets is a pretty unremarkable chapel, that is, if you can find it. Most of the joy of this chapel is the finding. As a result, I shall not include a detailed description of it's location within this guide, suffice to say it is near, but not actually at, Harwood Dale.

St Margaret's Chapel

Cost	Free	
Time	Allow half an hour	
Distance	8 miles, North West, Page 6	(30)

Hidden disused chapel buried in the countryside.

Once located, although it is not shown on present mapping, there is a footpath from the road across a small field and into the chapel, or rather what remains of it. The field occasionally contains stock and if you are not happy making the short crossing try again another day.

It is not difficult to understand quite why the chapel was abandoned, as it's location and lack of customers seem fairly difficult problems to surmount even for the most ardent churchgoer.

To quote from an 1848 guide book... *This little sanctuary is indeed almost inaccessible by carriage, and the chapel itself will not repay the labour with which it must be approached.* Well, in those early Victorian days this may well have been the case, but, today it is so very rare to find a place so completely deserted and uncommercialised that even local people are not aware of its presence that this church deserves a visit for that reason alone.

So now the history of this delightful little chapel.. Sir Thomas Posthumus Hoby, Knight of Hackness and M.P. For Scarborough was a local wealthy landowner and owner of the Hackness estate in which Harwood Dale resides. He was by all accounts a fine diplomat and spent a lot of his time in London tending to matters of state. His Wife, Lady Margaret remained on the Hackness estate and saw to the day to day running of a large country estate. Sir Thomas was her third husband and she wrote, the first of its kind, a diary of her day to day existence during the period she lived in Hackness. This can be found going by the title of "The Private Life of an Elizabethan Lady" and can be a difficult read. Sir Thomas erected the chapel in 1634 in memory of his wife for *"divine service for the good of the souls and bodies of the inhabitants dwelling withing Harwood Dale".* Of course, he might be a tad upset were he able to see it in its present condition.

The Lichgate (Entrance) circa 1840

Ravenscar

Approximately ten miles north of Scarborough can be found the small and rather well spread village of Ravenscar. Ravenscar is a small and unassuming village over endowed with history, but, with very little to show for it as far as the casual visitor is concerned.

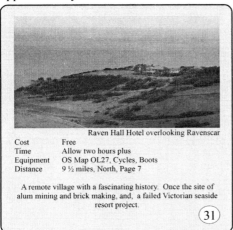
Raven Hall Hotel overlooking Ravenscar

Cost	Free
Time	Allow two hours plus
Equipment	OS Map OL27, Cycles, Boots
Distance	9 ½ miles, North, Page 7

A remote village with a fascinating history. Once the site of alum mining and brick making, and, a failed Victorian seaside resort project.

(31)

Ravenscar was the site of one of a series of Roman coastal signal stations stretching along the East Coast. During the construction of The Raven Hall hotel in 1774 workmen found a stone inscribed in Latin which translated indicated a fort and tower had been built in the reign of Justinianus.

The Raven Hall hotel stands majestically on the highest point of the cliff and although the construction looks defensive in nature the battlements are merely romantic early Victorian reconstructions. Early owners of the hall were involved in the Alum works situated just to the North of the hall.

Production of alum started in 1615 and continued for 250 years. Alum was an essential material extracted from shale for the cloth and dyeing trade, used mainly to fix dyes to stop them running. The alum was extracted from the shale in a very unusual manner. The shale was burnt in large heaps in the quarry and the chemical was dissolved out with hot water. The liquid then needed to be crystallised and this could only be performed by adding alkali. The only convenient form of alkali at that time was urine. Apparently, the urine was collected locally as well as being shipped in from London at a cost of 12 shillings a ton! The mixture was then evaporated in pans 9ft by 5ft. Imagine the smell! The author G.P. Taylor used this setting and location as the inspiration for his fictional best selling book 'Shadowmancer'.

Access to the beach (rocks) is by steep footpath alongside the Raven Hall. This area is renowned for fossils and you may come across fossil hunters following this somewhat treacherous path alongside you.

In Victorian times Ravenscar was planned out as a new seaside resort, even to the stage of marking out the plots and building the access roads for the new buildings. The plots were put up for sale but there were hardly any takers and the scheme folded.

More information is available at the small visitor information centre here and it is worth taking the time to read the exhibits carefully to appreciate just how this little village has changed over the centuries.

Cycling and walking is a popular here as there is direct access and free parking to the disused Scarborough to Whitby railway line. (see page29)

King Alfrid's Cave

From Scarborough at Ebberston in the dip take a right turn and park up in the trees near the sign for Chafer Wood. Follow the path up the edge of the wood (now owned and maintained by the Yorkshire Wildlife Trust) from the sign to a place hardly known about, even by locals.

King Alfrid's Cave

Alfrid Saxon king of Northumbria, died and was buried at Little Driffield in the year 705. There are conflicting reports of how he died and therefore below you will find two historical accounts of his death below.

From "Bulmers *History and Directory of East Yorkshire* 1892"

Cost	Free
Time	Allow 30 mins plus
Equipment	Boots for walking
Distance	10 miles, West, Page 6

(32)

Alfrid was an amiable and peaceful sovereign, who had spent much of his early life in the pursuit of learning in the monastery of Iona, and was afterwards known as Alfrid the Wise. There are conflicting accounts as to the cause of his death. William of Malmsbury says he died of a painful disease; but tradition avers that he was wounded in a battle at Ebberston, that he managed to escape from the field to the shelter of a cave hard by, whence he was removed next day to Little Driffield. The cave, which is now scarcely perceptible, has been known from time immemorial as Ilfrid's Hole.

From "Hinderwell's Scarborough 1798"

Upon the hill, above the house, is a small Cave, in a rock, called by the country people Ilfrid's Hole ; they inform the inquirer, from tradition of their ancestors, that a Saxon King of that name, being wounded in battle, fled from his pursuers, and took shelter in this cave, where he remained one night, and was next day conveyed to Driffield.

The following inscription, which was upon a stone over the Cave, and afterwards painted upon wood when the stone decayed, is remembered by some of the ancient inhabitants. " alfrid, King of Northumberland, was wounded in a bloody battle near this place, and was removed to Little Driffield where he lies buried :+ hard by, his entrenchments may be seen." An inclosure at the west end of Ebberston, adjoining the Pickering road, now known by the name of Bloody Close, strongly indicates that a battle has been fought there; but the tradition is, that alfrid was wounded in a battle within the lines of Scam-ridge, (either Six Dikes, or Ofwy's Dikes) near this place. This Cave is now almost filled up by the falling in of the rock ; but several of the old people of the village remember when it would have contained eight or ten persons

Sir Charles Hotham, about the year 1790, erected a plain building, of rude stones, in memory of this Saxon King alfrid, on the summit of the hill, within twenty yards of the Cave. It is of a circular form, the top terminating in a dome, with a narrow entrance to the inside, and might contain near twenty persons: the whole is surrounded by a dwarf wall.

Boggle Hole

Aside from being, perhaps, one of the winning contestants in an oddest village name in

Boggle Hole

Yorkshire competition, there is nothing remarkable to be found at Boggle Hole. A long mainly single track road leads to this bay from the main A171 Scarborough to Whitby road around 11 miles north of Scarborough.

However, there is an excellent, little known about, and free, parking area here that accommodates around forty cars and is superbly situated for walking along the coastal paths in this area.

Cost	Free
Time	As long as you like
Equipment	OS OL27 for walking or cycling
Distance	11 ½ miles, North, Page 7

(33)

Little known about bay and easy access to Robin Hoods Bay

Taking the road on foot down towards the beach sees you meeting up with the long distance coastal path The Cleveland Way. From here you can choose a variety of routes. Taking the path north brings you to the quaint, charming and unique village of Robin Hoods Bay after about half a mile. From here you can enjoy the delights of Robin Hoods Bay (see page 47) and then, subject to a favourable tide, take the return to Boggle Hole via the beach. Alternatively, if The Cleveland Way is taken to the south, it is possible to reach the fascinating failed resort of Ravenscar (see page 44) after around two miles. The return can be made via the ex Scarborough to Whitby railway line which is crossed via a bridge over which you hardly knowingly crossed, to get to Boggle Hole. This makes a return walk of around 5 miles. OS OL27 map is very useful for this short and scenic walk.

View towards Ravenscar from Boggle Hole

Boggle hole is also an excellent starting base for an off (or on) road cycling expedition with it's proximity to the ex Scarborough to Whitby railway line (see page 29) giving cycle access north and south as well as easy (although uphill) access west to the Yorkshire Moors.

Robin Hood's Bay

Despite the name of this quaint seaside village desperately clinging to the east coast cliffs, the well known man of Sherwood had nothing to do with this ancient coastal village. The village is perhaps one of the most scenic and photogenic places the visitor is likely to come across on the Yorkshire coast. Hundreds of small fishermen's cottages huddle together on the steep east facing cliffs not unlike nesting seabirds on a precipitous cliff.

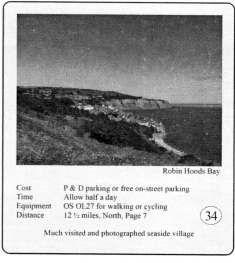

Robin Hoods Bay

The village can be split into two separate parts, the upper and the lower. It is not possible to drive to the lower part of the village. Pay and display parking is available at the upper part, or, free on-street parking can usually be found just a little further away from these car parks. Alternatively, it is possible to park at Boggle Hole (see page 46) or cycle in via the ex Scarborough to Whitby railway line (see page 29).

Cost	P & D parking or free on-street parking
Time	Allow half a day
Equipment	OS OL27 for walking or cycling
Distance	12 ½ miles, North, Page 7

(34)

Much visited and photographed seaside village

During the 18th century Robin Hood's Bay was a busy thriving fishing community with more than its fair share of the smuggling community. Given it's location it is not difficult to see why this was the case, as, any excise men visiting the village would be spotted well before reaching it, thus giving ample time for booty to be stashed in one of the many bolt holes, secret passages and hiding places. Indeed, it is said that a bale of silk could pass from the bottom of the village to the top without seeing daylight.

Gradual erosion by the sea has meant the village has crept closer and closer and eventually actually into the sea. In 1975 a sea wall was built to protect the village from the sea at a cost of just under £580,000. It is believed to be the highest sea wall in Britain standing 40 feet high and 500 feet long.

A National Trust visitor centre can be found in the Old Coastguard Station, near the slipway which is open June to September and has a small exhibition room explaining the geology of the area. Obscure shops can be found tucked away in the small streets and passageways and children and adults will enjoy exploring all these crooked ways.

One of the wider streets

Lilla Cross

Of the many stone crosses to be found on the North Yorkshire Moors, Lilla Cross is by far the most impressive. Said to be one of the oldest Christian monuments in the north of England it can be found at the highest point on Fylingdales moor some 12 miles north east of Scarborough.

Lilla Cross

The reason for including this cross in this book, rather than any of the others, is that it stands high and isolated on the desolate North Yorkshire Moors and requires quite some effort to reach. Once reached the views to be seen in good weather are long ranging and photogenically dramatic. If a visit can be timed to coincide with a summer sunset then even better.

Cost	Free
Time	Minimum of 4 hours depending on start point
Equipment	OS OL27 for walking or cycling.
	Foul weather & safety gear, Boots.
GPS co-ords	N 54° 22.581 W 000° 37.920
Distance	12 ½ miles, North west, Page 6

(35)

The cross is said to mark the grave of Lilla, an officer of King Edwin of Northumbria who died saving the life of the King by putting his body in front of an assassins sword thus saving the Kings life. Erected in about 625 it has been moved on several occasions and it is unclear whether the cross now resides at its original location. Right location or not, it is to be sure Lilla would have approved of its present location.

The writer's favourite route is by mountain bike starting from the parking area at Langdale End just to the east of Dalby Forest. Parking can be found either in the small village parking area or outside the Moorcock inn, whose facilities are a great refreshment on the return. The route is a long five and a half mile uphill drag through Langdale Forest and takes quite some time for all but the exceptionally fit. The pay off is the return journey which is five and a half miles downhill! This takes around a quarter of time it took to get up to the top.

From Langdale follow the road to the north west and take the first right outside the village (Sign posted Birch Hall). After this take the next right onto a gradually diminishing tarmac road up into Langdale forest and continue for another five miles on the rough track up through the forest, checking with your OS OL27 map regularly. When you pop out of the forest at the northern edge you will be alongside the Fylingdales early warning station and Lilla Cross will be visible to the north. Return via the same route.

Lilla Cross can be accessed by cycle or foot from other (probably easier) locations including May Beck car park at around (3 miles. see page 49), Hole of Horcum (5 miles. see page 52), A171 Scarborough to Whitby road by parking near the Flask (4.5 miles), A169 Pickering to Whitby road near Whinstone Ridge (4.5miles). Whichever route is taken it should be pointed out that weather conditions can change dramatically and quickly on these high moors and adequate safety and navigational equipment should be taken at all times.

Falling Foss and May Beck

Situated 14 miles north east of Scarborough can be found the delightful waterfall named Falling Foss and its associated stream, May Beck. Take the A171 main Scarborough to Whitby road and at Sneaton junction take the B1416 signposted to Ruswarp. After passing a small forested area on the right you come upon a sharp right turn in the road. At this point there is a junction of three minor roads with the B1416. You can take the first or the second. Both roads are marked as dead ends. The first (over a cattle grid) takes you to the May Beck car park, the second to the Falling Foss car park.

May Beck

Cost	Free
Time	Allow two to three hours at least
Equipment	Boots and OS OL27 map
Distance	14 miles, North West, Page 6

(36)

Ideal place for a walk followed by a picnic.

Which road you take is your own choice, but, the May Beck car park and picnic area is more open than the Falling Foss one which is shaded by tree cover and is a better choice for very hot days. This area has a wealth of walks and off road cycle routes and a detailed study of the OS OL27 map will assist in your choice of routes.

A simple easy walk that covers a return distance of just a mile and a half by foot is to walk alongside the river and wooded valley of May Beck to either Falling Foss or May Beck car park depending on where you parked in the first place. The path has no great gradients and is suitable for children who usually end up climbing a tree or two. Recent rainfall will make the path muddy in places. The path is part of the waypointed, long distance, 'Coast to Coast' route, which, takes you through the beck at the Falling Foss end, however, this short section can be easily bypassed for those with less that waterproof footwear.

The May Beck car park is also situated on the Moors to Sea cycle route and its is possible to do a small section of this long distance route. Following the route south from here will take the rider, or walker, high up onto Fylingdales moor and taking the path up to Lilla Cross (see page 48) and back makes a journey of around six miles. Make sure adequate foul weather equipment is taken as conditions can change rapidly up here.

Falling Foss waterfall

Thornton le Dale

One of the prettiest villages in Yorkshire can be found on the A170 15 miles west of

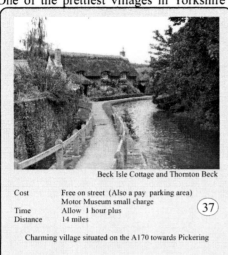

Beck Isle Cottage and Thornton Beck

Cost   Free on street (Also a pay parking area)
            Motor Museum small charge   (37)
Time   Allow 1 hour plus
Distance   14 miles

Charming village situated on the A170 towards Pickering

Scarborough. Thornton beck runs through the village and alongside the main road for a short while before disappearing off south towards the river Derwent. Parking is on the roadside is often difficult due to the popularity of this little village, however, there is pay and display parking to the south of the main road at a small charge per day. Next to the car park is a small pond with seating and some well fed ducks.

Prior to the 1920's the village was called Thornton Dale, the "le" was added around this time to try to improve the marketability of the village. The village has become a favourite stopping off place for locals who like to buy an ice cream and wander around the village absorbing the atmosphere of this quiet and pretty unspoilt area.

There are no tourist attractions, as such, to visit here, but just wandering around the village is a pleasure in its self. There is a small collection of interesting shops to browse,

or just follow the footpath by the river upstream for a gentle stroll. Take the path near the road bridge and you will see one of the prettiest, and most photographed, houses in the village, Beck Isle Cottage, with its rustic brick chimney pushing through the thatched roof.

Further on and up the hill take a wander around All Saints Church yard and find the beautifully carved celtic style cross. Also, take a little time to find the sad gravestone of Robert Simpson who outlived all of his nine children. A grim reminder of just how hard life used to be in those unhealthy times.

At the opposite end of the village on the road towards Pickering can be found an old petrol station that has been converted in one part to a small motor museum. Visiting the museum is by accompanied appointment and opening times are displayed. In front of the museum there is usually a collection of classic cars on the forecourt, some of which are for sale.

From here the ancient market town of Pickering lies only 3 miles to the west and Dalby Forest can be found 3 miles to the north. See page 57 and page 39 respectively.

Bempton

The three miles of coastline at Bempton are host to a huge array of nesting seabirds. Nestling closely to the 300 foot high chalk cliffs can found over a quarter of a million birds of many differing species. Puffins, Tern and Gulls as well as gannets, guillemots and kittiwakes. Bempton is 15 miles south east of Scarborough and the cliff access is signposted for the centre of the village.

The cliffs at Bempton

The area is a now a protected reserve administered by the RSPB. A large car park is situated on site together with an information centre and gifts shop. There are no entry charges to the reserve, however, car parking is pay and display. Various talks, walks and guides are planned throughout the year or guide books are available from the

Cost	Car parking charge
Time	Allow two hours plus
Equipment	Binoculars. OS OL27 map if walking
	Bird spotting book useful
Distance	14 ½ miles, South East, Page 9

(38)

shop. A pair of binoculars are useful, if only to blend in with the large number of enthusiastic bird watchers visiting the site.

Viewing platforms have been built overhanging the sheer cliff faces to enable visitors to view the birds in their natural cliff side habitat. Care should be taken when visiting the site and children kept under strict control for their own safety. Those with a fear of heights may need to stay away from the viewing platforms.

It goes without saying, that the best time to visit is the nesting season, however, whatever the season the cliff top views are spectacular and worth a visit at any time of the year. Best to avoid foggy days.

Before the practice was banned, it was normal for local people to harvest the eggs and every year groups of men would assemble at the top of the cliffs with large baskets and long ropes for this purpose. One would be lowered by rope whilst several others steadied the line as the collector swung from side to side picking eggs from the cliff on each swing. Although we now consider egg collecting abhorrent, this was considerably

Egg harvesting

more humane than the sport of shooting birds from the pleasure boats, for no other reason than target practice, which was also popular at these times.

The Hole of Horcum

As good a place as any to start a long or semi casual ramble is The Hole of Horcum. This natural ampitheatre is situated mid way along the A169 Pickering to Whitby road. A large free parking area is set just off the road.

The Hole of Horcum

Cost	Free (free parking area)
Time	Allow 2 hours plus
Equipment	Picnic. OS OL27 map if walking, Boots
Distance	14 ½ miles, West, Page 6

(39)

Legend has it that an angry giant, or perhaps the devil himself, scooped the earth out of the moors and cast it aside to form The Hole of Horcum and Blakey Topping respectively. Utter tosh, of course, but small children and animals are often impressed by the tale and it is a lot easier than trying to explain glaciation theory which is the real reason for the formation of this stunning landscape.

The Hole of Horcum is a very photogenic place and the scenery on these high moors is very dramatic, but, conditions can change rapidly from very clear to thick fog in a matter of minutes, it is therefore wise to ensure clothing and equipment is suitable for these conditions before setting out walking. OS OL27 map is required.

Suggested walks : For simple there and back walks try - Malo Cross or Newtondale Halt, where you can watch the North York Moors Railway winding its way through the base of the valley. Another walk, is to Levisham village, where you can refuel or re-warm in the village pub before returning. A stroll to the National Trust's Blakey Topping is worthwhile. This takes you to a mini mountain sat amongst the wild moors and forests. Or for a short walk, a quick jaunt down to the bottom of the hill to the Saltergate Inn and back can be very refreshing, if it is open!

Of course, all this area is now part of the North Yorkshire Moors National park which was created back in 1952 in order to preserve this area of outstanding natural beauty. Despite what most people believe the entire area is purely man-made and not natural in any way. Prior to Neolithic times the whole area was covered in thick forest and over a period of thousands of years man destroyed this forest entirely. It must have been a pretty popular area as burial mounds, standing stones, tumuli, dykes, settlements and enclosures can be found en masse and new discoveries come to light on a regular basis. It is possible to find examples of rock art all over this area once you acquaint yourself with exactly the type of stones to search for.

Nearby can be seen RAF Fylingdales, built in 1962 the base has primarily been used as inter ballistic missile early warning station. Originally it had three 40 metre "golf balls" which held the huge radar equipment, indeed, they even became a small tourist attraction in their own right. These have since been replaced by the triangular structures now seen.

Rudston Monolith

Situated at All Saints Churchyard in Rudston can be found a fascinating relic of prehistoric times in the form of a standing stone of quite immense proportions. Very little is known but much is hypothesized at just how this stone was placed in this position. It stands 26 feet high and is believed to extend a further 20 feet below the ground. Current belief is that it has stood here for over 4000 years and was erected as a meeting place or place of worship.

There are more questions than answers to this tale as although it is known the stone was at its present position in Roman times it is not known where the rock came from and just how it was transported to its current location since the stone is not from local strata.

Since you have found your way to the All Saints Church you may as well pop inside and have a look around. There is a well researched leaflet available inside the church explaining the history (of sorts) of the monolith.

Rudston Monolith

Cost	Free (Church donations)
Time	Allow 1 hour plus
Park	anywhere in village
Distance	14 ½ miles, South, Page 9

(40)

When finished in the church wander into the village itself and you will find one of the nicest Wolds villages you are likely to come across. Take time to find the course of the Gypsey Race and follow the path alongside it into the village. The Gypsey Race is a stream whose waters flow only intermittently and not necessarily after rainfall. The stream often springs into life after periods of long drought and it is not possible to predict when this may occur.

The reason for the unusual characteristics of this stream is probably due to the chalk deposits under which the Wolds sit which hold vast reserves of water in underground caverns. Underground pressures then force water up through the ground to burst out and form streams.

If you visit when the waters are flowing you will be treated to crystal clear stream waters, otherwise, a overgrown weed ridden dry riverbed will be your less than impressive reward..

The clear waters of the Gypsey Race

Goathland

The small moorland village of Goathland lies just 16 miles north west of Scarborough.

Filming in progress at Goathland

The route by road is around 25 miles but is well worth the effort required. Goathland has always been a quiet hidden haven of natural beauty but in recent years it has enjoyed increased popularity as a result of it being used as the location for the filming of the television series Heartbeat, and a small part in Harry Potter. Indeed many of the buildings used in the series have retained their on screen names.

Cost	Free or Pay Display car parking
Time	Allow three hours plus
Equipment	OS OL27 map for walking, Boots.
Distance	16 miles, North West, Page 6

(41)

Scenic moorland village often used as a film set.

There is no on-street parking in the main street, however, there is a small pay and display car park near the centre. Alternatively, parking on the verge is possible on the outskirts of the village near the Mallyan Spout Hotel to the south west of the village. The village itself is a long gangly affair and is a pleasant stroll on a hot summer day, if you are lucky you may catch sight of filming in progress.

The Railway station is worth visiting and is a main stop on the North Yorkshire Moors Railway, the country's most popular heritage railway, which run steam locomotives north to Grosmont and Whitby and south as far as Pickering. The line is run by a mixture of volunteers and paid staff and Goathland station is kept in a pristine retro condition that gives the impression time stopped around fifty years ago. The station was used in the Harry Potter films as Hogsmeade station.

To the south west of the village is the Mallyan Spout waterfall which nestles at the bottom of a tree lined hidden valley and well worth a visit. The waterfall can be accessed from several directions the easiest being to take the path down the side of the Mallyan Spout Hotel for an easy, but sometimes muddy, walk of around half a mile. It is possible to continue past the waterfall and onto Nelly Ayre Foss for a slightly extended walk.

Mallyan Spout waterfall

Flamborough

A visit to the area would not be complete without a trip to Flamborough Head. One of the most impressive landscapes on the east coast can be found in the area around the peninsula of Flamborough Head. Flamborough Head has been an important position since before Roman times and probably derived its name from 'flame' indicating its use for signaling. It is believed the Romans built and signal station here similar to the ones found at Scarborough, Filey and Ravenscar although no trace has yet been found, the most likely explanation being it was reclaimed by sea as a result of erosion many years ago.

The town itself stands just over a mile from the three coastal access points of North Landing, Selwick Bay and South Landing.

Flamborough Selwick Bay

Cost	Car parking charges – see text
Time	Allow 1-2 hours
Equipment	Boots, walks can be muddy in wet.
Distance	16 ½ miles, South East, Page 9

42

Three different bays to visit on headland of Flamborough

A pay and display car park at the road end facilitates access to the North Landing. The beach has a delightful small bay with a steep slipway. Here you will find the white chalky beach and, at low tide, access to a vast array of caves cut out by the action of the waves on the cliffs. As you would expect stories of smuggling and excise men abound here. After exploring the caves it is possible to take the coastal path south, about one and a half miles, to Selwick Bay. Alternatively, access via car is possible.

Selwick Bay has another pay and display car park and here you will find the light house, which can sometimes be visited, and another delightful bay similar to North Landing. From 1770 to 1806 over 174 ships were lost or wrecked in the area around Flamborough Head. As a result the lighthouse was built here in 1806. It is still in service and has been the saviour of many a sailor over the past 200 years.   The tower is 26 metres high and has a light which flashes four times in 15 seconds which can be seen up to 24 miles away. During fog the horn blasts twice every 90 seconds.   A earlier lighthouse can be seen on the roadside prior to the car park, although, there is no evidence that this was actually ever put to use. From here the coastal path goes north to the North Landing or just over two miles south west to the South Landing.

Flamborough Lighthouse

Sewerby Hall

Sixteen miles south east of Scarborough and just to the north of Bridlington can be found the parks, gardens and house of Sewerby Hall. This is one of the more expensive places to visit in this guide, however, it is included because from October until April entry is free. Car parking is free in summer.

Sewerby Hall gardens

Cost	Oct to April free. Otherwise charge per person.
Time	Allow 3-4 hours plus
Distance	16 ½ miles, South East, Page 9 (43)

A multi featured attraction with all day fun for children and adults alike. Not free in summer.

A super place to visit for children and adults alike the gardens have a zoo, ornamental and walled gardens, a sensory and rose garden, woodland walk, wood carvings and a courtyard craft section. There is a land train linking with Bridlington town centre which enables visitors to visit the town without having to find further parking, although there is an extra charge for this service.

The zoo is particularly popular with children as they are allowed to feed some of the domesticated animals. There is a walk through aviary and a large collection of birds sees Indian Blue Peafowl, Golden Pheasant and Temmincks Tragopan as well as a colony of Humbolt Penguins. Ponies, Llamas, Monkies and Wallabys are just a few of the diverse species to be seen here.

For the casual golfer there is a pitch and put or for the more keen a full eighteen hole golf course.

Llamas at Sewerby Hall

Building on the hall began in 1714 and further additions to the structure were made in 1808 and later. The hall houses various galleries and exhibitions which occasionally change during the year.

There is a permanent Amy Johnson exhibition which houses a large collection of memorabilia about this Hull born aviator who became the first (was there a second?) woman to fly solo the 11,000 miles from Croydon to Darwin in Australia in 1930. Sadly she died in an aircraft accident after crashing into the River Thames in January 1941.

There are all the usual facilities of a major attraction, disabled access, toilets and cafe facilities and it is quite easy to spend the best part of a day here without any difficulty.

Pickering

The small busy market town of Pickering lies 17 miles to the west of Scarborough and is well worth a visit. It is quite possible to spend a whole day wandering around the various museums and historical attractions the town boasts. Parking can be found in several pay and display car parks or for free parking, simply get lost in the side streets where ample on-street parking can be found.

Pickering railway station is the start of the North Yorkshire Moors steam railway and wandering around the beautifully maintained railway station it is usually possible to see a number of steam locomotives or you can take a return trip on the train itself (charges apply).

Pickering during WW2 weekend

Cost	Free back street or Pay an Display parking
Time	Allow half a day at least
Distance	17 miles, West, Page 6

44

Delightful unspoilt market town worth a visit on its own even if not visiting the other local attractions.

Near the town centre can be found the Church of St Peter and St Paul which has the most complete collection of medieval wall paintings in the country. Probably painted in the 1400's these were hidden under coats of whitewash for hundreds of years before being re-discovered in 1852, only to be whitewashed over again. Only in 1876 were they uncovered to be viewed by all (see page 58).

Further along Castlegate can be found, not unsurprisingly, The Castle. Owned by English Heritage this castle was originally built by William the Conqueror as part of his campaign to suppress the rebellious northerners. Various re-builds and additions have been made over the years with the castle falling into disuse in the 16th Century. A small, not unreasonable, charge is made for entry to the castle and grounds.

Near the railway station can be found the ever improving Beck Isle Museum of rural life. A small charge gets you into a fascinating display of life in times past. Superbly reconstructed rooms of shops and workshops bring Pickering's history to life in a way enjoyable for both children and adults. An award winning museum with all the usual facilities you would expect of such a museum.

On Hungate (Main A170) just to the west of the town centre can be found the deceptively large antiques centre. Not really a tourist attraction, but worth a visit, and you may find it difficult not to part with some of your 'hard earned' whilst browsing the huge array of collectibles and antiques. If you listen very carefully you will undoubtedly hear the phrase 'we chucked one of those out years ago!'

In the town centre (Market Place) can be found some typical market town shops, fortunately, this one of those disappearing town centres that has not been spoiled by an influx of high street stores, some of the shop fronts still retaining their Victorian elegance.

Church of St Peter & St Paul, Pickering

Tucked away behind old cottages just off Market Place can be found Pickering's parish

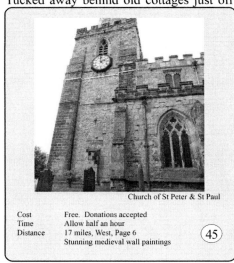

Church of St Peter & St Paul

Cost	Free. Donations accepted
Time	Allow half an hour
Distance	17 miles, West, Page 6
	Stunning medieval wall paintings

(45)

church of St Peter & St Paul. A truly remarkable church, due, to the fact it contains one of the country's most complete set of medieval wall paintings. There is no charge for entry, however donations and a particularly good printed guide to the church are available inside.

It seems likely the paintings were executed around 1450, but, as a result of Protestant Reformation they were covered over within a hundred years of them being painted. It was likely they would have been perceived as ostentatious and viewed as indication of a wealth of church at that time. Whatever the reason, they were purposely hidden and forgotten about until in 1852 workmen accidentally rediscovered them whilst removing plaster from the walls.

They were uncovered for a while and viewed by many visitors, but, the then vicar decided that the paintings were a distraction from his sermons and they were duly whitewashed over to be hidden from view once again. In 1876 during further renovations it was decided to uncover the paintings and restore them to their former glory.

In times before books and colour illustrated printing the paintings must have given inspiration and physical interpretation to the sermons of the day. Indeed how many times must the preacher of the day have pointed to The Descent into Hell to illustrate the

The Martyrdom of Edmund

consequence of sin. Freshly painted and complete, the effect must have been quite stunning.

One of the most graphical of the frescoes is The Martyrdom of Edmund, which tells the story of Edmund King of East Anglia, who, after his people had been murdered and pillaged by the invading viking Ivar, was demanded to surrender by Ivar. Edmund replied saying he would only surrender if Ivar gave up his heathen ways and followed a life of Christ. Not unsurprisingly, this did not go down too well with Ivar, who took the King, insulted him and beat with rods. He was then taken to a tree tied up and beaten with whips. He still failed to give in to the invaders and consequently was shot with spears until he looked like the bristles of a hedgehog. Finally he was beheaded and his head hidden in the forest.

Danes' Dyke

Danes' Dyke is huge ancient defensive structure stretching two and half miles cutting across the Flamborough headland some three miles from its tip. Reaching from Cat Nab on Bempton Cliffs in the north to Sewerby in the south and by using natural ravines and man made banks it provided a very effective protective boundary for those who built it.

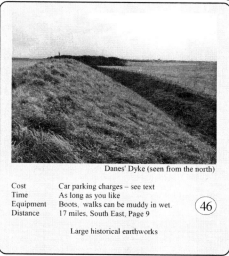
Danes' Dyke (seen from the north)

Cost	Car parking charges – see text
Time	As long as you like
Equipment	Boots, walks can be muddy in wet.
Distance	17 miles, South East, Page 9

Large historical earthworks

(46)

Despite its name, very little is known about who and when the dyke was constructed. The current thinking is that as a result of archaeological excavations completed during 1879 and 1919 when flints and stone age artefacts were found, the Danes did not build this dyke and it pre-dates those invaders by some two thousand years. However, this is by no means conclusive and the true story of Danes' Dyke is yet to be uncovered.

Most of the Dyke is on private land, however, it is possible to see the north end of the dyke as this cuts through the coastal footpath along the Bempton cliffs with access easiest from the RSPB reserve at Bempton (see page 51). (At the time of writing it was possible to walk along the top of the dyke for around half a mile at this point by use of a permissive path.) Driving along the Bempton to Flamborough road the dike can be seen about one and a half miles from Bempton.

The south end of the Dyke can be accessed by visiting the Danes Dyke pay and display car park via a long narrow driveway from the Flamborough to Bridlington road. This part of the dyke has been declared a nature reserve. From this point you have access to the woods and a woodland walk which wanders its way through gardens which were once the site of a grand house and have small wooden carved sculptures along the trail. Alternatively, a short walk takes you to the pebbly beach and there are paths to both Flamborough, Sewerby Hall (see page 56) and Bridlington. There are basic facilities here with toilets, a shop and picnic area which can all be found next to the car park.

This would make an excellent base for a day's discovery of the area. Car parking charges are pay and display at an hourly rate.

Danes' Dyke nature reserve

Malton Museum

Malton museum can be found in the centre of the town. There is pay and display parking

Malton Museum

Cost	Museum, small charge per person.
Time	Allow half hour for museum and another hour to walk to Orchards Fields
Distance	19 ½ miles, West, Page 8
	Visit in conjunction with Wharram Percy

(47)

alongside the museum or slightly out of the centre, free on street parking can be found fairly easily.

The old town hall in Market Place is home to this small but fascinating museum which has an exhibition of Roman artefacts found whilst excavating the Roman fort at Orchard Fields on the ground floor. On the first floor can be found the Wharram Percy exhibition both recreating and displaying the life and times of this lost medieval village (see page 61). Also, there is a social history collection relating to trade, local government, racing and other aspects of the town and surrounding area.

Malton, or Derventio as it was known, was an important place in Roman times with a fort and attached settlement being built here, possibly near to the crossing of the river Derwent. It is possible to visit the Orchard Fields area that was excavated during 1927-1930, around half a mile from the museum, where bumps, lumps and plaques explaining the site can be found. No less than six Roman roads have been traced heading into this fort which gives some indication of its importance within the Roman infrastructure. Orchard Fields is not the most exciting of archaeological sites and only really warrants a visit for those with a fascination of things Roman. Pompei it is not, and you are left feeling much more could be achieved on the site.

Site of Roman Fort, Orchard Fields

There is evidence to suggest that this area later became a royal villa for king Edwin in Saxon times, and here, the life of the king was preserved from an assassin, by his faithful Lilla. (See page 48)

Next to the Roman remains can be seen a building of obvious antiquity fronted on the road by a wall and three arched openings. These are the remains of a much larger manor house and estate constructed by Ralph, Lord Eure in the 16th century (in the reign of James I) which, after his death, passed to his uncle, William, who in turn left it to his two daughters. They, however, could not come to agreement on the use of the house and after a tedious and expensive lawsuit it was decided to pull the house down and the material shared. The process was carried out under the inspection of the High Sheriff and so scrupulous was the division that the stones were shared one by one. Some compromise appears to have been reached before the entire estate was destroyed as the lodge in front of the great house and the three arched gateway by the street are still remaining.

Wharram Percy Village

The Wolds of East Yorkshire are the site of many deserted villages most of which little trace can now be seen. Wharram Percy is one of these villages and it is no more remarkable than any of the others, with the exception that, Wharram has been the site of detailed investigations from 1952 to 1991. As a result the remains are open to the public for all to wander around and wonder at.

Wharram Percy is 20 miles from Scarborough and 6 miles south east of Malton. The car park is around half a mile from the village and the walk can be muddy in wet conditions. There is little left standing in the village with the exception of the church and some modern railway buildings. That said, the church is roofless and in a state of gradual decline and the railway no longer exists. Believed to be on the site of a roman road, the village

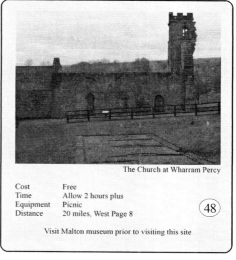

The Church at Wharram Percy

Cost	Free
Time	Allow 2 hours plus
Equipment	Picnic
Distance	20 miles, West Page 8

(48)

Visit Malton museum prior to visiting this site

buildings were originally constructed sometime between the 10th and 12th centuries, although it is likely the site has been occupied for much longer.

It is quite easy to miss the village buildings as you are drawn towards the church by the path. The village buildings are on a small plateau on the hillside to the north of the church. Some of the building footings have been uncovered but most are humps and bumps in the grass.

The reason for the demise of the village is now believed to be the result of sheep! Wharram survived the Harrying of the North and the Black Death but by the 15th century the need for sheep to supply the booming textile trades meant farmers were utilising every spare piece of land for the much more profitable raising of sheep. It also meant less jobs in the traditional arable farming and as a result the village de-populated naturally, with the final tenants being evicted by the land owner in 1517. The church continued to be used into the late 1800's until a new church was built at nearby Thixendale.

Most people visit Wharram Percy for the deserted village, but, there is a more modern and more neglected desertion here that of the railway. The Malton and Driffield railway line opened in 1855 and worked for over a hundred years eventually closing completely in 1958, prior to the Beeching cuts of the 1960's. Nearby it is possible to find the entrance to the 1.6km Burdale tunnel, another one of those magnificent pieces of Victorian construction that are currently laid to waste, it was bricked up in 1958. Ironically, those early 1950's archeologists will have been working alongside when the railway was in full swing and over the years will have witnessed the decline and dilapidation of the line, which, in some enthusiasts eyes, is more important than the site they were working on. Finds and an exhibition on Wharram Percy can be found at Malton Museum (P. 60).

National Railway Museum

Although outside the geographical borders of this guide The National Railway Museum has been included because of the vast size and national importance of this museum. The museum is based in the centre of the city of York which is around forty miles south west of Scarborough.

National Railway Museum

Cost	Free, although parking can be difficult
Time	All day
Equipment	Food for picnic area.
Distance	37 miles, West

Super day out in an outstanding museum (49)

The museum is open every day (except Christmas period) 10:00 to 18:00 and entry is free to all. There is car parking available at the museum, however, this can be expensive and visitors may find it cheaper to use the park and ride systems in operation . On-street parking is virtually impossible as it is covered by a by the residents only scheme.

Once inside, the visitor will find a huge collection of locomotives, over a hundred in fact, as well as over two hundred other items of rolling stock dating back to 1813. Exhibits include Rocket, Mallard and a Japanese bullet train. Particularly worth spending a little time on is Queen Victoria's carriage which has been perfectly preserved and shows the railway at its most opulent. Also on show is a collection miniature locomotives from various parts of the world. As well as other exhibitions covering all the differing facets of the railways and their equipment it is also possible to look around the workshops, where restoration projects currently underway can be viewed.

For children there is a miniature railway (well, perhaps adults as well) and a railway themed play area. The facilities are excellent, as you would expect from a world class museum. There are indoor and outdoor picnic areas within the complex which enables visitors to consume their own food.

Currently, the museum also has within its grounds the Norwich Union Yorkshire Wheel. This is a 54 metre high wheel similar in style to the London Eye. It has 42 enclosed air conditioned pods which can hold up to eight people and the ride offers spectacular views across the city of York and beyond into the Yorkshire countryside. The ride takes around 13 minutes and there is an extra charge per person. Wheelchair access is available for the ride.

Should you have any time left after visiting the museum a walk around the centre of York is well worth the effort. The history of York dates back to well past Roman times and the buildings in the centre of the city have managed to avoid the ruthless efforts of developers and retain their historic looks. The city is always buzzing with life as it is a major world tourist attraction and as you wander around you will hear many different languages being spoken. The city is flanked by ancient defensive walls which are freely accessible on foot and make an interesting tour around the city.

Mini Golf

It drives you nuts! There are a number of mini and crazy golf courses in our area and anyone with children will just love searching one of these out and having a go. Mini golf, and its themed brother, crazy golf, is one of the few games, if it can be called a game, that brings a level playing field to all players irrespective of age and ability, and, for a dad to be beaten by his four year old son is a pleasure and a delight to behold! Most of the courses listed below are only open during the summer season.

Scarborough crazy golf

Cost	Small charge per person. More expensive if balls lost!
Time	Allow 1 hour plus

Crazy golf, fun for all the family!

There is a British Minigolf Association which promotes mini golf, crazy golf and adventure golf in the UK and they regularly hold British and International tournaments.

Scarborough : In Scarborough there are three courses. A themed crazy golf can be found at Victoria Park on Peasholm road, opposite the Alexander bowls centre near the north bay and Peasholm park. There is easy parking next to the course.

A beautifully maintained mini golf course can be found hidden in Peasholm park itself. See page 21 for details on access and parking.

Another more relaxed mini golf course can be found alongside the Clock Tower on the South Cliff. Again, easy parking next to the course, and lots more to see in this area as well. For details see page 24.

Filey : A relatively new and excellently constructed sea themed course can be found on the promenade near the beach. Parking can be nearby in Church ravine or on Filey Country Park, see page 33.

Mini golf is available near the Filey Golf club, to the south of the town. Follow West Avenue from the town centre to a car park at the road end. The mini golf course is just a few yards from this car park.

Finally, a large mini golf course is located in Filey Country Park on top of the steep cliffs! See page 33.

Crazy Golf - Filey

Beaches

A trip to Scarborough would not be complete without a trip to the beach. There are several within easy reach of Scarborough and below you will find a quick guide to the more popular of these.

Scarborough south bay beach

Cost   Dependant on location
Time   All day

Scarborough & Filey have superb patrolled beaches which are
ideal for a full day outing.

Scarborough - North Bay Beach. A large sweeping north east facing bay from Scalby Mills in the north to Scarborough headland in the south. Parking along the marine drive gives easy access, or, parking at the Scalby Mills end gives access to the quieter part of the beach.

Scarborough – South Bay Beach. This is the most popular beach in the area with around half a mile of sands and a seafront area with amusements, shops and all the usual seaside trappings. The beach is cleaned by machine every morning to ensure it is kept tidy and litter free. Scarborough headland protects the south bay from heavy seas and as a result the water is excellent for bathing and paddling. Further along the bay towards Scarborough Spa the benefit of the protective headland is lost and this area is often in use by surfers. In summer lifeguards patrol the beach.

Cayton Bay. Three miles south of Scarborough can be found the uncommercialised Cayton Bay. Parking is possible in the pay and display car park found there. The beach is around one mile in length and has rocky sections at low tide. It is very popular with surfers as the bay generates good quality waves when the conditions are right.

Filey Bay. Without doubt the best beach in the area. Four miles of beach protected in the north by the natural promontory of Filey Brigg with easy access on foot or by car as well as for dinghies, canoes, windsurfers etc. The best area is from Filey Brigg to the south of Filey town. Parking is available in Filey town or on Filey Country Park (see page 33). A walk along The Brigg is a must but do check tides as it is easy to get cut off along The Brigg. Lifeguards patrol during summer.

Filey Beach looking north

There are other beaches mainly to the north of Scarborough but these are more difficult to access and are not generally used by the majority of visitors.

Fossil Hunting

The Yorkshire coastline in our area is often referred to as the Dinosaur Coast not because of the number of older people that choose to live here but because of the rich deposits of fossils that can be found on the beaches and cliffs. Already mentioned in the guide is "Walking with the Dinosaurs" which takes you to Jackson's Bay, one of the richest sources of fossilized remains in Scarborough. It is not possible to go into fine detail on the geology and various rock strata of our area as this would take up considerable space. A particularly good publication entitled "The Dinosaur Coast" is available locally which follows this route.

Fossil hunting around Scarborough

Cost	Dependant on location.
Time	Full day out, depending on location
Equipment	Boots, bag, geologists hammer,patience

The Yorkshire coast is an excellent hunting ground for pre historic remains.

Children particularly love fossil hunting and they are usually better at it than adults due to their sharp eyesight and nearer proximity to the ground. The richest sites for fossils are found between Scarborough and Whitby where good quality ammonites are fairy easy to come across.

In Robin Hood's Bay plenty of loose rocks can be found on the shore containing ammonites and belemnites. The rocks at Ravenscar are a little more difficult to access and take a more trained eye to find fossils. Plant fossil beds can be found at Hayburn Wyke, Scalby Ness, Yons Nab and, the much easier to access, Cayton Bay. Filey Brigg contains huge quantities of fossilised burrows as well as full blown fossils. There is one very large ammonite just at the end of Carr Naze, but very difficult to locate. Filey beach and cliffs contain loose fossils with many Gryphaea shell commonly known as Devil's toenail.

Amonite found on Filey beach

Further south along Filey Bay, at Speeton, can be found an area of shore where the red boulder clay recedes and is replaced by the grey Speeton Clay. The Speeton clay is extremely rich in fossil remains with huge quantities of belemnites amongst other fossils. The clay hides the fossils very well and they can be difficult to spot, however, once you have "got your eye in" they become much easier to locate. Many of the fossils are covered in iron pyrites (fools gold) which gives them a golden look. This area is very popular with hardened fossil hunters and so it can be difficult to find larger specimens as these are usually picked up pretty quickly. Access to the cliffs can be made from either the beach or Speeton village itself, with parking available near the church every day except Sunday. A small donations box can be found in the car park.

Cycling to Lilla Cross

66

Sunset on Filey beach

16.1,48.8/ 51.3,62.15/ 56.3,25.9,31.1,33.1/ 37.6,27.3,29.1,39.2